Praise for
COMEDIES FOR THE VIRTUAL STAGE

Virtual theatre started as a stopgap strategy to keep theatre alive when stages went dark. It has since blossomed into a new and easily accessible art form that offers playwrights, actors, and directors opportunities to sharpen their skills, hone their craft, and share their creative talents with audiences and one another. This collection of short comedies produced by the online theatre company *PlayZoomers* will introduce you to the pleasures and possibilities to be discovered in the world of virtual theatre, and entertain you each step of the way.

—**DONALD STEVEN OLSON**
award-winning playwright of *Oscar and Walt*,
and *The Christine Jorgensen Show*

Virtual theater brings performance to anyone with a computer and an internet connection. This anthology is ideal for college acting courses, training students in live, online, and hybrid modes. The creative challenges are just as compelling — and often more budget-friendly. *PlayZoomers* are pioneers of performance's future and these plays are the perfect gateway. Whether for class or experimentation, this collection unlocks new possibilities for actors and audiences alike.

—**ANSLEY VALENTINE**
Associate Professor and Head of Acting-Directing
Indiana University - Bloomington

From the theater at Epidaurus to the laptop screen, play production may have evolved, but our need to laugh at the human condition is unchanged. These twenty plays hold up a funhouse mirror to human nature, delivering classic comedy in a new medium. They empower everyone with a computer and a connection to produce theatre and bring the hilarity home.

—**CHRISTOPHER BYRNE**
theater critic, author of *A Man of Much Importance: The Life and Art of Terrence McNally*

COMEDIES FOR THE VIRTUAL STAGE

COMEDIES FOR THE VIRTUAL STAGE
Copyright © 2025 by Janet R. Carpman and Mary Ann Hubbard

All rights reserved under the Pan-American and International Copyright Conventions. This book may not be reproduced in whole or in part, except for brief quotations embodied in critical articles or reviews, in any form or by any means, electronic or mechanical, including photocopying, recording, or by any information storage and retrieval system now known or hereinafter invented, without written permission of the publisher.

Cover photo credits:
Photos from PlayZoomers' productions.
Top left: Morgan Duncan in *A Horse! A Horse!* by Steven Otfinoski, directed by Bari Biern. Top right: Laura Hubbard in *A Snake with a Ladder*, by Nick Maynard, directed by Brad Van Grack. Bottom left: Devin May in *The Audition*, by Steven Otfinoski, directed by Joshua Secunda. Bottom right: Alice Simon in *Curtain Call*, by Greg Hatfield, directed by Sabrina Carmichael.

Library of Congress (LOC) Number: 2025944523

ISBN (paperback): 978-1-968919-04-7
ISBN (ebook): 978-1-968919-05-4

ARMINLEAR

Armin Lear Press, Inc.
215 W Riverside Drive, #4362
Estes Park, CO 80517

COMEDIES FOR THE VIRTUAL STAGE

SHORT PLAYS ADAPTABLE FOR ONLINE PERFORMANCE

EDITED BY
JANET R. CARPMAN AND MARY ANN NICHOLS

ARMINLEAR

CONTENTS

INTRODUCTION   1

COMEDY SCRIPTS
   A First-Draft Second-Rate Love Story by John Busser   11
   A Horse! A Horse! by Steven Otfinoski   29
   A Snake With a Ladder by Nick Maynard   43
   Almost Perfect by Trevor Suthers   61
   Armchair Critic by Nicky Denovan   75
   Can You Hear Me Now? by Morey Norkin   91
   Chemistry Date by Lenny Hort   101
   Curtain Call by Greg Hatfield   111
   Drummer Boy by Lisa Dellagiarino Feriend   125
   Imperfectly Frank by Seth Freeman   137
   I've Got a Bun by Cary Pepper   153
   Santa Noir by James McLindon   167
   Speed Dating by Curt Strickland   181
   Talkback by Sam Graber   195
   The Audition by Steven Otfinoski   207
   The Holiest of Sacraments by Patricia Connelly   217
   The Noir Before Christmas by John Minigan   233
   Tree #2 by R.A. Pauli   249
   Your Call is Important to Us by Janet R. Carpman   261
   Your Favorite by Ken Green   285

EDITORS & CONTRIBUTORS   303

ACKNOWLEDGMENTS   311

INTRODUCTION

As with other performing arts, theatre has always been characterized by innovation — in playwriting, acting and directing training and methods, costuming, makeup and hair, set design and set dressing, props, lighting, sound and music, projections, and more. Despite this ongoing evolution, the model for how theatre is presented has been relatively consistent over time. With a few exceptions, including videotaped, filmed, or live-streamed onstage productions, theatre is typically performed live in front of an audience.

Starting in 2020, the COVID-19 pandemic had a chilling effect on live theatre in the US and around the world. The close, physical interaction of actors and backstage crew and the seated proximity of audiences became hazardous during a time when the virus was not yet well understood and vaccines were not yet available. Between 2020 and 2023 — the official years of the pandemic[1] — there was a massive shutdown of gathering places for education, work, recreation, worship, commerce, and culture, including theatre. Some theatres laid off staff, some paused their productions, and many closed permanently. According to *American Theatre* magazine, this constituted a "crisis of contraction."[2]

WHY PRODUCE ONLINE THEATRE?

When theatres were shut down during the pandemic, another avenue emerged that took advantage of the digital technology of the time: online theatre produced through online streaming. This way, theatre artists could still write, direct, and act, and audiences could still experience dramas, comedies, and other genres without exposing themselves to an infectious and potentially deadly disease.

NPR's Scott Simon reflected on the importance of the arts during the pandemic and afterward:

> There is much daily loss and suffering in America right now. It may seem elitist to worry about the future of the arts when so many people struggle for food, work, and health care. But the arts can fire minds, warm souls, dazzle, and delight. We will want them to be there in times ahead, for us and especially for our children. As Ashley Wheater told us, "Live art, the magic of the theater, is one of the few things that can bring total strangers together in unique harmony, reminding us of our humanity.[3]

One of the surprises we have experienced as producers of online theatre — "this new art form," as one of our directors dubbed it — is its wide appeal and compelling benefits, even in non-pandemic times.[4] Here is some of what we've learned over the last five years:

ONLINE THEATRE CAN BE STREAMED LIVE.

There is a certain thrill to acting in or watching live theatre. Online productions can be live, which adds to the intensity of the storytelling and the feeling of connection between the audience and the actors.

ONLINE THEATRE CAN HAVE HIGH PRODUCTION VALUES.

With close attention to digital technology, online theatre can have excellent visuals and sound. This technology involves the actors' cameras and microphones, the technical director's stitching together of intro/outro videos and sound cues for a given play, and the quality of virtual backgrounds (via the use of green screens and ring lights).

ONLINE THEATRE HAS LOWER PRODUCTION COSTS THAN ONSTAGE THEATRE.

Both onstage and online theatre incur costs for licensing, artist and crew compensation, costumes, props, marketing, and more, but onstage theatre is typically a much more costly proposition. Performance venue rent and overhead, live tech, lights, sound, sets, and set dressing are just some of the additional expenses involved. Online productions may have shorter runs and thus lower

INTRODUCTION

fees for licensing, as well as artist and crew compensation. They will also incur costs of video conferencing technology and other expenses, but these are likely to be quite low by comparison.

ONLINE THEATRE CAN BE AN EFFECTIVE TEACHING TOOL FOR DRAMA STUDENTS.

Drama teachers can easily use video conferencing technology to allow students to try out works by various playwrights, scripts representing different genres and themes, and a wide range of acting roles. Instructors can rehearse scenes and produce entire plays (either live or recorded) online at a very low cost. By definition, students can participate remotely, which makes virtual productions viable if students are not able to attend classes in person.

ONLINE THEATRE PROVIDES WORK FOR THEATRE PROFESSIONALS.

There are usually too few opportunities to keep playwrights, directors, actors, production designers, and other theatre professionals fully employed. In addition to providing more directing and performing jobs, online theatre can also spark learning: sharpening acting and directing skills, exploring how to use digital technology for performing, figuring out methods for showing scenery, enhancing productions with curated royalty-free music and sound effects, and more.

ONLINE THEATRE OFFERS THEATRE ARTISTS NEW OPPORTUNITIES FOR CREATIVITY.

Creating plays on a nontraditional platform means inventing a new theatrical vocabulary: how to convey the essence of a character online, how to visually and emotionally connect actors in different locations, how to create realistic or abstract scenery, how to use video to integrate graphic design and music to introduce plays and scene changes, etc.

ONLINE THEATRE ENABLES DIRECTORS, ACTORS, AND CREW WHO ARE NOT IN THE SAME LOCATION TO WORK TOGETHER.

While some theatre professionals travel to be part of a particular play, the cast and crew in onstage productions need to be in the same place. A significant benefit of online theatre is that theatre artists who live in different places and would not otherwise meet, let alone work together, can participate in the same play.

ONLINE THEATRE PROVIDES ACCESS TO AUDIENCES WHO CAN'T ATTEND ONSTAGE THEATRE.

Would-be audience members may not live near a theatre. They may not drive or have public transportation available. Local weather conditions may discourage some people from traveling to see a play. Older patrons and those with mobility disabilities may find it difficult to walk to the theatre from parking or public transit. They may also find it challenging to negotiate stairs or narrow aisles once inside.

ONLINE THEATRE IS MORE AFFORDABLE TO ATTEND THAN ONSTAGE THEATRE.

Pricing for Broadway productions, national tours, and regional theatres has climbed beyond the means of many audience members. With lower overhead, online theatre ticket prices are typically much more affordable. Online theatre audiences do not need to pay for transportation or parking, and low-cost snacks are close at hand.

ONLINE THEATRE OFFERS AUDIENCES A LOW-RISK OPPORTUNITY TO DIP THEIR TOES INTO NEW OFFERINGS.

At a price likely to be in line with a movie ticket, online theatre offers a low-risk opportunity to audience members who want to taste new or unfamiliar plays, but are not sure they want to make a meal of them. While watching at home, if they don't find the performance interesting or appealing, they can privately turn off a play, rather than making a public exit from an onstage theatre.

ONLINE THEATRE OFFERS AUDIENCES A CLOSE-UP VIEW OF ACTORS NOT ALWAYS POSSIBLE IN ONSTAGE THEATRE.

Watching a live, onstage play from Row ZZ of the Orchestra or the heights of the Balcony enables audiences to view all the action, but not always see the actors' expressions. Online theatre is more intimate: watching it on a TV screen, computer monitor, or digital device enables audiences to see facial expressions more clearly.

INTRODUCTION

ONLINE THEATRE ENABLES PLAYWRIGHTS TO SEE THEIR PRODUCED PLAYS WITHOUT NEEDING TO TRAVEL.
Much as they would like to see every production of their work, logistics of time and money prevent many playwrights from being able to travel to see their work produced on domestic and international stages. Online productions enable them to easily and inexpensively view their plays.

ONLINE THEATRE CAN FOSTER A SENSE OF COMMUNITY SIMILAR TO THAT OF ONSTAGE THEATRE.
Multiple rehearsals and detailed discussions about characters, backstories, props, tech, and the particulars of a given play often lead to camaraderie among producers, playwrights, directors, casts, and crew members. Some have called this a sense of "community" or even an online theatre "family."

WHAT DOES IT TAKE TO PRODUCE ONLINE THEATRE?[5]
While there is no single foolproof recipe for producing online plays, there are certain recommended ingredients.

VIDEO CONFERENCING TECHNOLOGY
Platforms such as Zoom™, Microsoft Teams™, Google Meet™, and others make it possible for audiences to see actors' live online video feeds simultaneously. This accounts for the magic of virtual performances. These platforms make audiences feel as if they are watching actors on the same virtual stage, regardless of the actual locations of the audiences and actors. We expect continuing innovations in video conferencing technology and hope that online theatre will benefit over time from new features and platforms.

Our online theatre company, *PlayZoomers*, uses Zoom™ to separate audiences ("Attendees") — who can watch performances but can't speak or be seen — from actors ("Panelists") who are seen and heard. This platform enables actors to control some characteristics of their audio, in addition to toggling their microphone on and off, and some characteristics of their video as they enter and exit the screen.

Zoom™ also allows actors to use "virtual backgrounds," which can serve as stage sets.

Virtual backgrounds, used in conjunction with green screens, enable actors to seem as if they are actually in the settings suggested by the script. A graphic designer can supply high-resolution images that can provide an almost infinite variety of virtual backgrounds.

Videos, featuring graphics and integrated royalty-free music and sound effects, can be created and run by a Technical Director to introduce a play ("Intro"), conclude a play ("Outro"), and depict transitions of time and space between scenes ("Interscene").[6]

EQUIPMENT

Additional equipment helps optimize the quality of video images and sound.

<u>External web cameras</u> ("webcams") work with computers to provide sharp, clear video images.[7] They usually have the added benefit of an internal microphone for improved sound quality.

<u>Green screens</u> optimize video image quality, especially when virtual backgrounds are used. They help avoid the distortion that may otherwise ensue. Green screens should cover the entire area behind the actors.

<u>Ring lights and other lighting</u> enable actors to be seen clearly. Ring lights often have settings to adjust lighting color and intensity. It is useful to have separate lighting for the green screen.

COSTUMES AND PROPS

As with onstage productions, costumes help establish the mood of the play and the particulars of the characters, and props can help bring the script to life.

Costume considerations for virtual theatre include avoiding patterns (such as stripes) that may "confuse" the camera and cause image distortion. Costumes should not use colors similar to those in the virtual backgrounds or green screens, so that actors are easy to see.

If props will be virtually "passed" from one character to another, each character must have an identical prop. Prop passing in online productions involves a particular "sleight of hand" technique that, ideally, will look real to an audience.

INTRODUCTION

THEATRE ARTISTS WITH TECH-RELATED SKILLS

In live onstage productions, crew members typically ensure that set changes occur at the right moment, lighting highlights the scenes, actors' voices can be heard by the audience, and wardrobe changes happen seamlessly. In an online production, a production designer and director will determine the look and feel of a play in advance and rehearse with the actors to make sure things go smoothly. But alone in their home studios, online actors need to be ready — not only to interpret their characters and relate to their scene partners — but also to operate the video conferencing controls (such as turning cameras and microphones on or off in a split second), set up their virtual backgrounds, change their costumes, position their props, etc.

EXTENSIONS OF THE LIVE PERFORMANCE

Recordings

Online theatre productions can usually be recorded; the technical requirements for doing so vary among different platforms. Recordings can be used as a rehearsal tool and even as an emergency backup in case a live production runs into snags due to weather, power outages, etc. Video recordings can also be edited, as desired, to document/archive the live event.

Accessibility

Accessibility features of video conferencing platforms enable everyone to use them.[8][9][10] Features vary among platforms and are likely to improve over time. For instance, Zoom™ offers automated closed captioning at the click of a button.

Curtain Calls

Directors can orchestrate curtain calls for virtual productions as they would for onstage plays. Actors and crew can return to the virtual stage after the "Outro" and introduce themselves to the audience.

Talkbacks

In a post-production talkback, the cast, crew, and audience members who wish to do so may come onscreen simultaneously to discuss the play(s), pose questions, and share observations. Zoom™, MS Teams™, and Google Meet™ all have "Q&A" features that enable participants to write comments and questions, which the hosts can manage and respond to.

WHAT MAKES A SCRIPT SUITABLE FOR ONLINE PRODUCTION?

In a word: simplicity. This assumes, of course, that the play is well-written with intriguing characters and believable dialogue. Let's break this down:

SIMPLICITY OF CHARACTERS

Ideally, an online production will keep the number of characters small (between one and four) if they appear on screen at the same time. More than six characters may be confusing for the audience; it isn't always clear who is speaking if there are too many "actor boxes" on the screen.

SIMPLICITY OF ACTION

Passing a prop or two is relatively easy; using identical items, actors can make exchanging props believable. However, it is challenging to orchestrate physical moves (such as hitting or bumping into other people or furniture) and physical intimacy. A clever director and technical director might find a way to make these actions work online (perhaps inserting slides, videos, or sound effects), but if the plot relies heavily on physical interaction, the play is probably not a good choice for virtual production.

SIMPLICITY OF LOCATION

Virtual backgrounds (sets) are wonderful tools and can be changed by the actors. However, if a play needs multiple virtual backgrounds, this can prove cumbersome for the performers. Even if an actor is technically astute, changing backgrounds can divert their attention from their scene partners and the character they are portraying.

INTRODUCTION

SIMPLICITY OF MUSIC AND SOUND EFFECTS

Currently, online technology doesn't easily accommodate scripts that require music. If the music is stand-alone (that is, no characters need to speak or sing while the music is playing), it may work. However, if two characters speak or sing simultaneously, the live audio effect is usually garbled. There have been some improvements in this area, but they aren't yet advanced enough to rely upon.

Sound effects (SFX) are easier to insert. As with any technical component, SFX require rehearsals with actors and the technical director. Rehearsing timing cues is critical since there can often be some lag time in online productions as audio/visual cues are launched.

HOW WE CHOSE SCRIPTS FOR THIS ANTHOLOGY

Each script in this collection was produced by *PlayZoomers* between 2020 and 2025. From the scores of plays representing a variety of genres and themes, we selected twenty comedies that would work best for performers and directors looking to gain experience with virtual theatre. Each script has well-drawn characters, believable dialogue, economy of setting, costumes and props, clarity of purpose, and, of course, humor.

PLAYZOOMERS, A LIVE ONLINE THEATRE COMPANY

While most virtual productions happen occasionally, in 2020, we founded a nonprofit theatre company devoted exclusively to live online theatre.[11] As of mid-2025, *PlayZoomers* had produced more than 139 online plays involving hundreds of playwrights, directors, actors, and audience members from 35 states and countries around the world.

PlayZoomers currently presents six ticketed online performances per year, featuring original plays of different genres, themes, lengths, and cast sizes. Productions include backgrounds (real or virtual), lighting, sound effects, music, video, props, and costumes. Each online performance is given twice, on weekend evenings, and is recorded. Our plays offer closed captioning and accessible playbills. Live talkbacks follow each performance.

It takes considerable effort to produce and publicize these plays. Producers, an executive director, technical directors, a graphic designer, a production associate, a website administrator, and a social media manager work throughout the year, guided by the *PlayZoomers* Board of Directors.

PlayZoomers trains directors regarding the ins and outs of online directing, regularly holds table reads for playwrights developing new work, and consults with organizations wishing to improve the quality of their virtual productions or readings. We partner with another nonprofit on an early childhood literacy program, "Act Me a Story," working with professional actors and directors to produce storybook videos for under-resourced preschool children.[12]

We seek creative ways to make use of our online productions. For example, we licensed one recording as a training tool for caregivers and another as a themed presentation at a statewide conference. We have worked with a writer to turn a screenplay into an online play that can be used as a teaching tool for Grades 6-12. We joined forces with a university drama department to create a purpose-built stage and live-stream a play. We welcome innovative ideas for using virtual theatre to benefit education, entertainment, work-related training, and other realms.

HOW DOES AN ONLINE PLAY LOOK AND SOUND?

Before you delve into the comedy scripts in this anthology, you might want to experience one of them on video. You can use the link below to see our production of *The Audition* by Steven Otfinoski, directed by Joshua Secunda, and featuring actors Gary Giurbino, Devin May, and Mary Ann Nichols. https://youtu.be/CnEHAa96i1g

References
1. "When did the Pandemic Start and End?" https://www.nm.org/healthbeat/medical-advances/new-therapies-and-drug-trials/covid-19-pandemic-timeline#.
2. https://www.americantheatre.org/2023/07/24/theatre-in-crisis-what-were-losing-and-what-comes-next/
3. Scott Simon, Host, NPR Weekend Edition, Dec. 12, 2020.
4. For reflections on online theatre by playwrights, directors, actors, and audience members, see https://www.playzoomers.org/celebrating-our-100th-play
5. For a useful discussion of the nuts-and-bolts of producing online theatre, see "A How-To Guide for Virtual Theatre" by Pioneer Drama Service (2020). https://www.pioneerdrama.com/pdf/VT_Howto.pdf
6. To show videos during an online production, you can use "Share Screen" in Zoom™, "Share Content" in MS Teams™, and "Present Now" on Google Meet™.
7. Laptops may have their own web cameras, but we've found that external webcams usually provide superior quality images.
8. Accessibility features on Zoom™ https://www.zoom.com/en/accessibility/faq/
9. Accessibility features on MS Teams™ https://support.microsoft.com/en-us/office/accessibility-tools-for- microsoft-teams-2d4009e7-1300-4766-87e8-7a217496c3d5
10. Accessibility features on Google Meet™ https://support.google.com/meet/answer/7313544?hl=en
11. https://www.playzoomers.org
12. https://washtenawpromise.org/videos/act-me-a-story/

A FIRST-DRAFT SECOND-RATE LOVE STORY

JOHN BUSSER

Reprinted by permission of the author.
For performance rights, contact John Busser, johnbusser@hotmail.com

Synopsis
Will our lovers (one-handed stevedore, John, and multiple-named ingenue, Vivian/Miriam/Marian) find the love that's eluded them for so long, or will Vivian's shocking past prove too much? Stay tuned for another exciting updated draft, which may or may not answer those questions.

Time
Early evening

Characters
JOHN/ACTOR 1, male, 20s-50s

VIVIAN/MIRIAM/ACTOR 2, female, 20s-50s

OLDER MAN/DAD/BRAD/TOM/ACTOR 3, male, 30s-50s

MOM/ACTOR 4, female, 30s-50s

STUART/WRITER male, 20s-50s

Setting
An empty theater stage

Estimated run time
13 minutes

A FIRST-DRAFT SECOND-RATE LOVE STORY

*[Note: Dialogue **(bold)** is delivered in a stereotypical soap-opera-ish way. Other dialogue (non-bold) is what the actors playing the character are saying to the unseen writer and to each other.]*

At lights up, JOHN and VIVIAN face each other, their profiles to the audience in a classic lover's clinch. Each holds a script in hand that they will refer to as they go.

JOHN
Oh, Vivian...

VIVIAN
Oh, John... I look at you and wAnder...

JOHN / ACTOR 1
(pointing at the script in his hand)
"Wonder..."

VIVIAN
Oh, John... I look at you and WONDER...

JOHN
Wonder what, Vivian?

VIVIAN
Oh, John. I wonder whether this will be like the other times you came back home here to Boundless Hope Manor.

JOHN
What do you mean, Vivian? "Other... times"?

VIVIAN
Yes, John. The "other times." Times where you arrived from your world travels, blowing into town on the cold Venezuela winds...

JOHN / ACTOR 1
(pointing at the script in his hand)
They're not cold. My script says hot.

VIVIAN / ACTOR 2
Sorry.

JOHN
Vivian, this time is different. I'm here to stay.

VIVIAN
(turning away from him, dramatically)
That's what you said the last time you were here… And the time before that… And the time before that… And the time before THAT… John, how many more "times before that" can I take before I lose my fragile mind?

JOHN
Dearest heart, I would sooner lose another one of my arms than hurt your mind. Honest!

VIVIAN / ACTOR 2
You say that now, John, but soon you'll…

Stops acting, looks past the audience.

Um, Stuart? Sorry. I have a question.

From behind the audience, STUART, the writer, steps up.

STUART
(he calls ACTOR 2 by her real name, whatever it is)
Yes_____?

ACTOR 2
I know this is still a work in progress —

A FIRST-DRAFT SECOND-RATE LOVE STORY

STUART

Yes, and just let me say thanks to you and *(name of the theatre where this is being performed)* for agreeing to do this read-through for me. I'm still working out some of the kinks. What's your question, sweetheart?

ACTOR 2

It's just that… well, Vivian's dialogue is a bit, you know, repetitive. "Time before that, time before that, time before that…" It just seems like maybe I should drop one of those…? Maybe?

STUART

Okay, first off *(ACTOR 2's real name)*, let me say you two are doing wonders with this script. I'm astonished by what you're bringing to it.

ACTOR 2

Thank you.

STUART

I don't know of any other actors who could do to this material what you two are doing to it.

ACTOR 2

Is that… good?

STUART

What do you think?

He waits a long beat. They stare at him uncomfortably.

Of course, it's good! It's breathtaking! I can hear the passion oozing all over the stage. It's better than I dared hope. BUT… as to your question, allow me to explain. Of course, Vivian would repeat herself. She's making a point, you see? Making… a point! Just as I am now making a point by repeating "Making a point." Her repeats are making the point that John never stays very long. The number of repetitions mirrors the number of times he left. Does that clear it up?

ACTOR 2
Oh, yes. It does! Thanks, Stuart!

STUART
Don't mention it. Now, if we could carry on…

ACTOR 1
Sorry, Stuart, I had a question too…

STUART
Oh yes, of course, *(he calls the actor by his real name)*. Go on…

ACTOR 1
So, John says on page six, "I would sooner lose another one of my arms than hurt your mind." Which is fine, except John talks about losing an arm.

STUART
He was using hyperbole. Like, *(adopting a made-up voice)* "Your breath is AMAZING!" or "If I don't get this job, I'll come back and KILL you all!" You know, that kind of thing.

ACTOR 1
And that's totally fine except… why does he say… "Another arm"? Makes it sound like he lost one already.

STUART
He did.

ACTOR 1
He did?

STUART
Yes, he did.

ACTOR 2
(shows script)
It's right here, at the top of one, see? The description says "JOHN, a one-armed stevedore, fresh from another of his many orca hunts in the waters off Venezuela."

A FIRST-DRAFT SECOND-RATE LOVE STORY

ACTOR 1
(looking at his script in puzzlement)

Um, my script doesn't say that.

STUART
It doesn't?

ACTOR 1
No. It just says "JOHN, a man home from a long sea voyage." Doesn't say how many arms he has, so I'm going to assume it's two.

STUART
OH! Oh, oh, oh, oh, oh! I am SO SORRY. You have Draft number 1, don't you?

ACTOR 1
Yes, that's what it says.

ACTOR 2
Wait! Mine says Draft 4.

STUART
Damn! I am such a Mindless Mickey! I was making some changes to Draft 4 and was using Draft 1 to check some things. I must have inadvertently mixed up the copies when I put the final scripts together. You're working with two different versions.

ACTOR 2
That's not good. Do you think we should stop and fix this?

STUART
NO! I am already so far behind on my revisions! I need to do this reading tonight to work out some problems. We'll just have to soldier on.

ACTOR 2
But what about —?

STUART
Please! We really do need to move forward on this. I will assume, as actors, you are smart enough to make the proper adjustments as we go. I was told you two are some of the finest actors in this entire area, including the children's theater. At least that's what it says on your Facebook pages.

ACTOR 1
I think we can tackle this, don't you, *(calls ACTOR 2 by her real name)*?

ACTOR 2
I'm ready if you are, *(calls ACTOR 1 by his real name)*!

ACTOR 1
Alright! Let's do this!

ACTOR 2
From where we left off?

ACTOR 1
Sure.

ACTOR 2
We're ready when you are, Stuart.

STUART
Thank you. Just let me get to the back of the house, and you go whenever you're ready.

STUART exits to back of house.

VIVIAN
You say that now, John, but soon you'll be off again on another of your mad orca hunts.

JOHN
Water parks pay top dollar for those beautiful, but deadly to the noble seal, swimming sea-beasts, Vivian. I thought you understood, I'm doing this for you.

VIVIAN
For me?! But you know of my work with Greenpeace. I can't condone what you've done! I love those swimming sea-beasts you speak of, and even though the seal population is doing just fine right now, I still don't want you risking it all just for me. Especially in light of... YOUR DISFIGUREMENT!

She points pointedly at his missing arm. ACTOR 1, who unfortunately has both arms, quickly hides one of them behind him to simulate the missing appendage. STUART applauds from the back, in awe of this acting choice.

JOHN
But my arm... longs to hold you, in my... arm. *(looking to STUART, questioning this)*

STUART
(from back of house)

KEEP GOING!

JOHN
... And I don't care if I AM disfigured. I figure my disfigurement won't figure into our plans.

VIVIAN
You have plans, John? To what? Sweep me off my feet? How? How can you sweep with only one hand?

ACTOR 1
Hand? I thought it was an arm?

VIVIAN
If only you were A whole... *(she checks the script)* ... man. I could love your wholeness.

JOHN
Miriam, what are you saying?

VIVIAN / MIRIAM / ACTOR 2
I'm saying…

Miriam? *(she looks out)*

STUART
(from back of house)

I changed the name! JUST KEEP GOING!

MIRIAM / ACTOR 2
I'm saying I love your whole, man!
I love his hole?

ACTOR 1

Should that be MY line?

STUART
(from back of house)

FOCUS PEOPLE!

JOHN

Oh, Vivian… *(BIG Sigh)* **MIRIAM**.

MIRIAM
John, I know I should look past your missing arm… hand… whatever. But what about…?

JOHN

What about who… Miriam?

At that moment, an older man enters.

OLDER MAN
What about ME, Miriam?

JOHN and MIRIAM turn as one to the OLDER MAN

JOHN
Brad!

A FIRST-DRAFT SECOND-RATE LOVE STORY

MIRIAM

Dad!

OLDER MAN

That's right! Me!

JOHN

Miriam, you called Brad "Dad"!

MIRIAM

He is!

JOHN

Brad is your dad?

MIRIAM

He's not Brad! He's Dad!

JOHN

But Brad's your ex-fiancé!

MIRIAM

He's my dad!

JOHN

Your dad is your ex-fiancé?!

MIRIAM

No, John. Pay attention. According to *(indicates the script)* Brad is not my dad! Tom is!

JOHN

Who's Tom?

OLDER MAN / ACTOR 3
(paging through his script)
Yeah, who's Tom? I'm *(real name of ACTOR 3)*.

MIRIAM
You are, Daddy!

OLDER MAN / ACTOR 3
But... but... but, my name is Bill... I think.

STUART
(from back of house)

What Draft number!?

ACTOR 3
Number 3! I'm the father, right?

STUART
NO! Sorry, I thought it was more intriguing to have an ex-fiancé enter the picture! I killed off the parents one draft back!

ACTOR 4
(from offstage)

GODDAMIT!

An older woman walks onstage carrying a script. She throws it down.

ACTOR 2
Who are you?

ACTOR 4
I was your fucking Draft 2 Mother!

STUART
(from back of house)

SORRY!

ACTOR 4
(yelling from back of house as she exits)

BITE ME, ASSHOLE!

A FIRST-DRAFT SECOND-RATE LOVE STORY

ACTOR 2
(to herself)
Boy, this script needs a lot of work…

JOHN
Miriam, somehow, you got engaged to your dead Father. When did THIS happen??!

MIRIAM
No, John, Brad was not my dead dad when he was Brad. I mean, first, he was my dad, but once he died, something told me he was someone I should be engaged to. He became Brad.

JOHN
"Something told you"?! And what was that, Miriam, hmmm? What was that?!

MIRIAM
(she waves the script in his face)
Draft number 4, John.

JOHN
(disgusted)
And I was going to give you my whole… *(he turns away, dejected)*

ACTOR 3
(whispering and indicating MIRIAM)
Hey, can one of you tell me if I'm supposed to ground her or kiss her?

JOHN
Hey, you can't kiss her, Dad! I mean, Brad! She's with me now!

MIRIAM
It's true! I can't be your fiancée or your daughter anymore. I'm with John now.

BRAD
Oh yeah! Well, I've got two hands. What's he got that I haven't?

MIRIAM
A name that hasn't changed in four drafts!

JOHN
Miriam, do you really mean it? Can you still be with a man with only one of these? *(he holds up his good right hand)*

MIRIAM
I'll be your good right hand, John.

JOHN
But it's my left one. *(waving left hand, pulled into his sleeve so it looks like a stump)*

MIRIAM
(giggling)
Oh, John, your sense of humor is so disarming…

All ACTORS stop and look out at STUART. They grimace.

STUART
(grumbling)
Fine, I'll take that line out!

BRAD
But Miriam! I love you! If there's not even a chance for me now, then why am I here?

JOHN
So I could fight you for the hand of the woman we both love! *(he holds up his right hand)*
Arm wrestle?

BRAD
Wait, Miriam! I can SHOW you how much I love you! And in a way that HE never will!
(he holds both arms out as wide as possible as if measuring) See? THIS much!

A FIRST-DRAFT SECOND-RATE LOVE STORY

JOHN
(only able to hold out one arm, the sleeve of the other drooping down)
Hey, no fair!

MIRIAM
Sorry, Brad, but I'm done with your bragging and your over-exaggerating. Eight inches, my ass!
(dramatically turning to JOHN) **You truly do love me, don't you, John?**

JOHN
More than I love orca hunting on the cool Venezuelan seas, my flower!

MIRIAM
Hot!

JOHN
Beg your pardon?

MIRIAM
They're hot seas, John. In my script, it says… "hot."

JOHN
(looking in his script)
Mine too, Marian.

MIRIAM
Miriam…

JOHN
Miriam.

MIRIAM
Now we're on the same page, sweetie.

She cuddles him. He puts his arm around her.

JOHN
So, it appears as if true love has won the day, m'lady. What say the two of us walk off into the sunset hand-in-arm-or-stump, while I tender my resignation as chief orca hunter, and prepare to settle down here in Bottomless Pit Harbor with the woman of my dreams.

MIRIAM
I think the place is called…

JOHN
(interrupting her)
I don't give a shit, Liz, Viv, Mallory, whatever your name is. I don't care where we are, who you are, who anybody here is. All I know is you're my gal, and I have a feeling that no matter what happens to us in any future drafts, if this writer wants to get asses in seats, he better give us one hell of a happy ending. Unless, of course, he wants me to put my Draft 2 stump up his ass.

MIRIAM
(shouting to the back of the house)
Do you hear that, Stuart? John and I want a happy ending. We want a big wedding, with hundreds of people there, fireworks, and a live band. I want a white dress that costs thousands and a special fitted tux for John with a place for a hook hand. And we want to live happily ever after in a house with a stream in the back and where it never rains except for when we want it to, which should be easy to suggest with a painted backdrop since I know that'll strain the budget. We want all that in the next draft, or we don't come back, and you can write about Brad and my mom getting together, so you'd have to bring her character back.

STUART
(rushing up)
That's it! That's my ending! I didn't see it until now.

JOHN
You mean it, Stuart? Will Miriam and I find true love and happiness in your next draft?

STUART
Yes, John! You and Miriam will live happily ever after. In Draft number 7!

BRAD
And what about me, will I finally have a character I can call my own?

MIRIAM
I'm sure you will, Brad.

STUART
I think I'm going to change his name to Tom. It's a good name. I hate to waste it.

BRAD
No, Stuart. I want to be Brad now. Brad is a good spin-off character name.

STUART
But that's my decision. Isn't it?

BRAD
In fact, I have a whole slew of ideas for my backstory. I see Brad as having been in the Coast Guard, fighting for whale rights, when he meets this young, fresh-faced kid named John. And he remarks, "Oh, you've got two arms, I see. You'll go far in this man's navy…"

BRAD and STUART walk off arguing, their words fading out as they go

JOHN
C'mon Miriam. This piece is already too long as it is. Let's go before we reach the end of this page.

MIRIAM
Oh, John, you always did know how to exit a scene.

JOHN
I've been doing it for many drafts now. You get to be an old hand at it. Even when you only have one. *(he holds up his stump)*

JOHN and MIRIAM exit laughing the laugh of two fictional lovers as they walk off into the sunset, just narrowly missing the end of the page.

Blackout

END OF PLAY

A HORSE! A HORSE!

STEVEN OTFINOSKI

Reprinted by permission of the author.
For performance rights, contact Steven Otfinoski, sotfinoski@outlook.com

Synopsis
King Richard III is in desperate need of a horse in the Battle of Bosworth Field. Horse dealer Sam Smedley comes to his rescue... or does he?

Time
1485

Characters
CATESBY, male, 20s, a supporter of Richard

RICHARD III, male, 30s, King of England

SAM SMEDLEY, 40s-50s, horse dealer

Setting
Bosworth Field, England, where Richard's army is engaged in a fierce battle with an army under the command of the Earl of Richmond, Henry Tudor.

Estimated run time
12 minutes

A HORSE! A HORSE!

CATESBY rushes in, speaking to Lord Norfolk, who is offstage.

CATESBY

Rescue, my Lord of Norfolk! Rescue, rescue!
The king enacts more wonders than a man,
Daring an opposite to every danger:
His horse is slain, and all on foot he fights,
Seeking for Richmond in the throat of death.
Rescue, fair lord, or else the day is lost!

RICHARD III, complete with humpback, enters brandishing a sword.

RICHARD

A horse! A horse! My kingdom for a horse!

CATESBY

Withdraw, my lord; I'll help you to a horse.

RICHARD

Slave! I have set my life upon a cast,
And I will stand the hazard of the die.
I think there be six Richmonds in the field;
Five have I slain to-day, instead of him. —

CATESBY exits at a run.

A horse! A horse! My kingdom for a horse!

SAM SMEDLEY enters.

SAM

Somebody call for a horse?

RICHARD
(turning to face SAM, sword ready)
I did! Be ye of the House of York or the House of Lancaster?

SAM

Neither.

He holds out a business card. RICHARD takes it.

RICHARD
(reading)

"Sam Smedley of Sam's House of New and Pre-Owned Horses." You're a... stableman?

SAM

That's right, Governor. Now about this horse...

RICHARD

Yes! I need a horse. At once!

SAM

Then I'm your man.

RICHARD

Good! Where's the horse?

SAM

One thing at a time, Governor.

RICHARD

Time? I don't have time! Can't you see I'm in the middle of a major battle here?

SAM

Oh, sure. I know. You Yorks and Lancasters. Always fighting and killing each other. With us poor locals caught right in the middle. Frankly, we're fed up with all your feuding, Governor.

RICHARD

Stop calling me Governor. I'm the King!

SAM

King Edward?

RICHARD

No! He's dead. King Richard.

SAM

Pardon me, Sire, but which one?

RICHARD

Which what?

SAM

Which Richard?

RICHARD

Richard the III!

SAM
(trying not to stare at Richard's hump)
Oh, yes. You're the one with the…

RICHARD

With the what?

SAM

You know… with the, uh…

RICHARD glowers at him.

Never mind.

RICHARD

Cease your prattle! Where is the horse?

SAM
(pulling out a small notepad and pencil)
You'll get it, Your Highness. As soon as we've taken care of a few details.

RICHARD
Damn the details. My kingdom hangs in the balance!

SAM
Sure it does. But so does my business. I've got to make a living too, you know.

RICHARD
All right, all right! But be brief, man.

SAM
Now, this horse you need… were you looking to buy or just rent?

RICHARD
What?

SAM
You see, Sire, I can rent you a nice, strong steed for a week at a very good rate. The day rate is cheaper but may end up costing you more.

RICHARD
I'll buy the horse!

SAM
A very wise decision, Your Majesty.

RICHARD
Now, where is it?

SAM
Hold on. There's the matter of size and color to discuss.

RICHARD
I don't care what *color* it is! I just want a BIG, STRONG steed!

SAM
Well, that's a rather general description, but I think I can fill the bill. Now you mentioned going into battle. For our customers who ride their horses into combat, we highly recommend battlefield insurance.

A HORSE! A HORSE!

RICHARD
What?

SAM
It's in case the horse should be injured, or God forbid, killed in combat. If so, you get back your full investment.

RICHARD
I don't want any insurance! I just want a horse!

SAM
I must say I think that a rather unwise decision, what with the high mortality rate of horses in battle these days. But you're the customer. Now there's just the little matter of payment.

RICHARD
See the Lord of the Treasury tomorrow. He'll pay you in full.

SAM
I'm afraid it's a bit more complicated than that, Your Kingship. *(beat)* Remember what you said.

RICHARD
What did I say?

SAM
I wrote it down right here. *(reads from notepad)* "A horse! A horse! My kingdom for a horse."

RICHARD
I said that?

SAM
Yes, you did indeed, Sire. And more than once, I might add.

RICHARD
You thought I meant that I would give my kingdom for a… horse?

SAM

Yes, and I took you at your word, your Worship.

RICHARD laughs.

RICHARD

Now look here, my good man. When I said that, I was speaking figuratively. Not literally.

SAM

I'm afraid you've lost me, Sire.

RICHARD

Let me explain. When I said "my kingdom for a horse," I was speaking in hyperbole.

SAM

Hyper-what?

RICHARD

Hyperbole. It's a kind of… exaggeration. Like when you're hungry and you say, "I could eat a horse." You don't mean you could actually <u>eat</u> a horse. You just mean you're extremely hungry.

SAM

I don't know about that. My cousin Zeke ate a horse once. Everything but the tail. Did it on a bet. Of course, he was drunk as a lord at the time.

RICHARD shakes his head. This is getting too complicated.

RICHARD

Look. I'll give you a hundred gold ducats for the horse.

SAM

You said your kingdom.

RICHARD

Be reasonable, man! I can't give you my kingdom! That's preposterous!

A HORSE! A HORSE!

SAM
All right, then. How 'bout half?

RICHARD
Half my kingdom? *(long beat)* Here. I'll tell you what I'll do. You give me the horse, and I'll give you… a quarter of my kingdom.

SAM
Which quarter?

RICHARD
You can have Wales and Northumberland.

SAM
I've got family in Northumberland.

RICHARD
There you are then!

SAM
It's on the wife's side. They're a terrible lot. They find out I've got a kingdom and they'll be moving into the castle quicker than you can say Jack Robinson. I'd never be rid of 'em.

RICHARD
But you'll be the king! You won't have to put up with that.

SAM
You haven't met my mother-in-law. No, Northumberland's out.

RICHARD
Then, how about Wales and Dorset?

SAM
Not Dorset. The wife doesn't like the sea air. Makes her break out in hives.

RICHARD

Shropshire?

SAM

Too windy.

RICHARD

Durham?

SAM

Too cold.

RICHARD

Cheshire?

SAM

Too much cheese.

RICHARD

Too much <u>cheese</u>?

SAM

The wife's allergic to cheese. One nibble and she blows up like a balloon. Ugly sight.

RICHARD
(at his wits' end)

Do you want a quarter of my kingdom or not??!!

SAM

Now don't get peevish. After all, you're saving the best parts for yourself.

RICHARD

IT'S MY KINGDOM! I'M THE KING!

SAM

All right, all right! Forget Wales. Forget it all. I'll take the hundred ducats.

A HORSE! A HORSE!

RICHARD

Now you're talking sense!

> *He grabs the notepad from SAM and scribbles on it, then tears out a page and hands it to SAM.*

Give this to the Lord of the Treasury tomorrow, and you'll get your money.

SAM

That's all fine and good, Your Holiness. But I'd like the cash now if you don't mind.

RICHARD

You think I'd go into mortal combat with a pocketful of ducats?

SAM

I suppose not. *(mulls it over)* All right. Seeing as how you're the king and all, I guess you're good for it.

> *SAM tucks the slip of paper into a pocket.*

RICHARD

Fine! Now, where's my horse?

SAM

I'll bring him round to you directly.

RICHARD
(looking around Bosworth Field)

You mean he's not here?

SAM

You think I'd be so daft as to be wandering around a battlefield leading a horse? No, Sire. Snowball is safe and sound back at the stables.

RICHARD

Snowball?

SAM
Pure white. To match the white rose of York.

RICHARD
That's just... lovely. But I need that horse now!

SAM
Now don't get yer chainmail in a tangle. I'll fetch him for you.

RICHARD
How long will that take?

SAM
Oh, I'll be back with Snowball before you know it. Half an hour tops.

RICHARD
Half an hour! I could be dead by then!

SAM
And what about me? I've got to cross this whole bloody battlefield. You can sit here and... hide under a rock.

RICHARD
I'm not going to hide under a rock! I'm going to stand my ground like a king!

SAM
Suit yourself. Those Lancasters will spot you in a second, standing here, what with your...

RICHARD
With my what?

SAM
(motioning awkwardly with his hands)
You know. That... thing.

A HORSE! A HORSE!

RICHARD

What thing?

SAM

The, uh, you know...

RICHARD

Are you, by any chance, referring to my <u>hump</u>?

SAM

Well, now that you mention it, it is a rather prominent part of your person, wouldn't you say?

RICHARD
(has had enough)

That's it! <u>That's it</u>! Keep your precious SNOWBALL! Keep your stable and every flea-bitten nag in it! Keep the hundred ducats! I'm going to win this fight on my own two feet! Just watch!

He runs off, brandishing his sword.

Richmond! Richmond! Where are you, Richmond?

SAM
(looking off at RICHARD)

Watch out, sire! Ooo! No! Behind you!

He covers his eyes and then looks through his fingers.

Oooh!

SAM heaves a deep sigh, takes out the slip of paper, and tears it in two. He begins to exit, then turns and looks off.

Hmm. Lord Richmond appears to be on foot. Snowball, old boy, I think we're still in business.

He starts to exit towards Richmond.

Uh, Your Highness! May I be the first to congratulate you?

END OF PLAY

A SNAKE WITH A LADDER

NICK MAYNARD

Reprinted by permission of the author.
For performance rights, contact Nick Maynard, nick.maynard.uk@hotmail.com

Synopsis
A retelling of the Adam and Eve story.

Time
The beginning of time

Characters
EVE, female, the first woman, and wife of ADAM, the first man

BRIAN, a malevolent serpent

ADAM, male, the first man, and husband to EVE, the first woman

GOD, an omnipotent being (Can be a voiceover)

Setting
The Garden of Eden

Estimated run time
10 minutes

A SNAKE WITH A LADDER

EVE stands by a tree (or a representation of a tree) featuring a dangling apple, just out of reach.

A snake [called BRIAN] enters.

BRIAN
Hello.

EVE
Hello — who are you?

BRIAN
I'm Brian.

EVE
And what are you then?

BRIAN
I'm a snake.

EVE
Nice.

BRIAN
And you?

EVE
I'm Eve... I'm a <u>woman</u>.

BRIAN
And what do you do then, Eve?

EVE
Cleave — mostly... I do a lot of cleaving.

BRIAN
Cool.

EVE
Is it?

BRIAN
I don't know...

EVE
To tell you the truth, I'm not a hundred percent sure what cleaving actually is.

BRIAN
It's clinging.

EVE
Oh?

BRIAN
(beat) Don't you get bored — cleaving?

EVE
I don't know... Maybe? What's bored?

BRIAN
You know — when you get fed up — jaded... When it feels like every day is the same as the day before.

EVE
Yes, I get the bored... I get so the bored...

BRIAN
It's just bored... Not "the" bored.

EVE
Still — it's good to know there's a word for it.

BRIAN
Doesn't Adam get bored, too?

EVE
No — I don't think so… He spends most of his time talking to God and giving stuff names.

BRIAN
Don't you get to name stuff?

EVE
No — apparently, I'm just the "bone of his bone and flesh of his flesh." So I can't give stuff names… Although I have given Adam and God a few… Usually, I just hang out, and Adam tells me about all the cool stuff he and God have been up to.

BRIAN
Don't you feel left out?

EVE
I never thought about it… But yeah, I do.

BRIAN
You need friends.

EVE
What are those?

BRIAN
People you can hang out with that aren't Adam.

EVE
What are people?

BRIAN
Of course, I forgot — it's just you two, isn't it?

EVE
Yeah.

BRIAN
Then you should get a hobby.

EVE
What's that?

BRIAN
Something you can do on your own when Adam's busy with God.

EVE
I go for walks... Look at stuff.

BRIAN
Sounds nice.

EVE
It is.

BRIAN
What sort of stuff do you look at?

EVE
Trees — grass... (*pointing to the apple hanging in the tree*)... that.

BRIAN
That?

EVE
Yeah — It looks nice.

BRIAN
It's an apple.

EVE
That's an apple...

BRIAN
You should try it.

EVE
No, I can't... God said we shouldn't eat those.

BRIAN
Why not?

EVE
No idea.

BRIAN
Are you sure God said you couldn't eat apples?

EVE
Positive... He said we can eat fruit from the trees in the garden — but "you must not eat the fruit from the tree that is in the middle of the garden, and you must not touch it, or you will die."

BRIAN
That's a bit dramatic... Is this the middle, though?

EVE
Yeah... I measured it in paces the other day... And the day before... I measure it most days to be fair...

BRIAN
Why?

EVE
I think it's my hobby... Measuring...

BRIAN
Why not... But are you sure... God and Adam could just be saying that to stop you from eating it because they want all the apples for themselves...

EVE
You think?

BRIAN
Possibly.

EVE
Well, that's not very fair, is it?

BRIAN
Not at all... I think that's why they've put them up so high.

EVE
The bastards!

BRIAN
You know that word, then?

EVE
What?

BRIAN
It doesn't matter... You should try one.

EVE
No.

BRIAN
Just one... One's not going to hurt, is it?

EVE
You don't think?

BRIAN
It's your right... You live here too. Why should Adam and God get all the apples?

EVE
You're right.

BRIAN
I bet it's because they taste like chocolate.

A SNAKE WITH A LADDER

EVE

What's that?

BRIAN

You'll find out in time...

EVE

But it's so high up, how am I going to reach it?

BRIAN

Well, you're going to have to work at it... What comes easy to Adam will never come easy to you — or your daughters... It's a metaphor.

EVE

I thought it was an apple.

BRIAN

It is — and when you eat it, your eyes will be opened, and you will be like God, knowing good from evil.

EVE

I still can't reach it.

BRIAN

You need some help... (*produces a ladder*) It's a leg-up... Put your foot on the first rung of the ladder... This is your first step to enlightenment and equality... Ascend to the...

EVE

...What's a rung?

BRIAN

That's a rung.

EVE

EVE climbs the ladder to get the apple

Yes... Yes... That's it... Take what is rightfully yours.

EVE comes down the ladder and takes a bite from the apple.

BRIAN

Well?

EVE

I don't know — I just expected it to taste better than this... It's not a pineapple, is it?

BRIAN

No... But it's the fruit of the tree of knowledge.

EVE

I suppose... (*beat*) Bit chilly, isn't it?

BRIAN

We've had good weather all week — it could be taking a turn for the worse.

EVE

Actually...

BRIAN

What?

EVE

I feel a little underdressed.

BRIAN

That's fine — you can get clothes... You'll love clothes — and shoes... Shoes and matching bags... You'll love them. It will be your thing... That and makeup.

EVE

Makeup?

A SNAKE WITH A LADDER

BRIAN

It's a thing — you'll understand later… But for now, you could sew some fig leaves together to cover your modesty.

EVE

I will.

EVE starts collecting leaves as BRIAN exits. ADAM enters.

ADAM

Eve?

EVE

Adam?

ADAM

What are you doing?

EVE

I'm fashioning clothes.

ADAM

What are those?

EVE

It will take too long to explain. *(gives him the apple)* Eat this.

ADAM

What is it?

EVE

It's an apple.

ADAM

We're not supposed to eat the apples.

EVE

Don't argue with me, just eat the fucker!

ADAM takes a bite.

ADAM

Eve?

EVE

What?

ADAM

You're naked... I'm naked. Fuck! Why did you do this to me?

EVE

Do what?

ADAM

Make me eat that.

EVE

Don't blame me for this... If anyone's to blame, it's Brian.

ADAM

Who's Brian?

EVE

The snake.

ADAM

You've been talking to a snake?

EVE

Yes.

ADAM

Why?

EVE
Why not — you weren't here — I got bored, and chocolate hasn't been invented yet.

ADAM
What's bored? And what's chocolate?

EVE
It doesn't matter. I need stuff to do.

ADAM
And talking to a snake called Brian, is that it?

EVE
Why not? A girl needs friends.

ADAM
Friends?

EVE
And hobbies.

ADAM
Hobbies?

EVE
Stop repeating everything I say.

ADAM
But I don't know what you're talking about.

EVE
That's because you're a man.

GOD appears.

GOD
What is this you have done?

ADAM

You tell him.

EVE

You're his mate — you tell him.

ADAM

Eve made me eat an apple.

GOD

She did what?

EVE

Thanks for that, you — grassing me up to God, you twat!

GOD

Because you have done this — you are cursed above all livestock and all wild animals!

EVE

Great! That's your fault, that is... God?

GOD

No — I don't want to hear from you... (*to ADAM*) You should have kept her away from the ladder.

ADAM

I don't know what that is.

GOD

You're an idiot.

ADAM

Thank you, God.

EVE

That's not a good thing.

ADAM

How do you know?

EVE

I don't know — maybe I took a bigger bite than you did... No, see it's stuck in your throat — Adam's apple's stuck.

GOD
(to EVE)

From here on in, you will have pain in childbearing — and with painful labor, you will give birth to children.

EVE

That's not fair.

GOD

And your desire will be for your husband, Adam.

EVE

This fool?

GOD

And he will rule over you.

EVE

I don't think so.

GOD
(to ADAM)

Because you listened to your wife — and ate fruit from the tree about which I commanded you — cursed is the ground because of you.

EVE

He's really pissed.

GOD
Through painful toil, you will eat food from it, all the days of your life. It will produce thorns and thistles for you, and you will eat the plants of the field. By the sweat of your brow, you will eat your food until you return to the ground, since from it you were taken — for dust you are, and to dust you will return.

ADAM
Can I just say it was more her than me? I never gave her no ladder — she did that herself.

GOD
You are both banished from this Garden of Eden, and you will nevermore have my ear or my love.

GOD disappears.

ADAM
Oh, please, God!

EVE
Great — that means you're gonna be hanging 'round here a lot more — getting under my feet... Just as I discover friends and hobbies. Typical... Now I need to find something to numb the pain. Brian? Brian? How can I get something that will return me to a state of ignorant bliss?

BRIAN appears.

BRIAN
(producing a bottle of Prosecco)

Behold, Prosecco!

ADAM
What about me?

EVE
What about you?

ADAM
Do I get anything?

EVE
You heard God — get to work — I need clothes, shoes, and handbags — and that shit don't grow on trees.

BRIAN
Amen, sister.

EVE
I like you... You're very smooth.

ADAM
I feel something.

BRIAN
Is it jealousy?

ADAM
I don't know what that is... I don't like feelings.

BRIAN
(to audience)

And so it begins.

END OF PLAY

ALMOST PERFECT

TREVOR SUTHERS

Reprinted by permission of the author.
For performance rights, contact Trevor Suthers, trevsuthers@gmail.com

Synopsis
A short, unromantic comedy with two young principals, Sean and Shannon, on a date that ends badly. No matter how hard you try, nobody's perfect, right?

Time
Present

Character Breakdown
SEAN, 20s-30s. Over-eager. Lacking in confidence.

SHANNON, 20s-30s. Self-assured. Temperamental.

Setting
Set in a cafe/pub/restaurant – table and two chairs, menus, a book

Estimated run time
10 minutes

ALMOST PERFECT

SEAN

You know something…

SHANNON

Yes?

SEAN

You know what you are, don't you…

SHANNON

What?

SEAN

You're perfect.

SHANNON

Don't be silly.

SEAN

No, you are, you're perfection itself.

SHANNON

Nobody's perfect.

SEAN

That's what I would have said before I met you.

SHANNON

You're being ridiculous.

SEAN

No, really, you're flawless.

SHANNON

You wouldn't say that if you knew me better. Believe me, I have plenty of flaws.

SEAN
None that I've ever noticed.

SHANNON
You can't say anyone's flawless; we all have our faults, we all have things about us, little quirks that annoy other people. We've only known each other a week. Just give it time, and I'm sure there'll be plenty of things about me that will start to irritate you.

SEAN
You could never irritate me. In fact, I can't believe my luck in meeting you. You're just perfect in every way.

SHANNON
Stop it now. Anyway, I don't believe you. What about me always being late? We've had three dates so far, and I've kept you waiting every time.

SEAN
I don't mind waiting. I'd wait forever for you, really I would.

SHANNON
No, you wouldn't, but if we carry on seeing each other, I guarantee you'll get lots of practice.

SEAN
We are going to carry on seeing each other, aren't we?

SHANNON
Of course, we are.

SEAN
Oh, thank goodness, for a minute there…

SHANNON
No, I really like you.

SEAN
You do?

ALMOST PERFECT

SHANNON
Of course, I do.

SEAN
I adore you.

SHANNON
You're so sweet.

SEAN
Not as sweet as you.

SHANNON
Oh, I'm not so sweet as you think I am.

SEAN
From where I'm sitting, you couldn't possibly be any sweeter.

SHANNON
You're still claiming you can find no fault with me? None whatsoever?

SEAN
That's what I'm saying.

SHANNON
Oh, I know something, here's an annoying little quirk of mine, bound to get on your nerves — twirling my hair. I'm always doing it — I'm doing it now.

SEAN
Your hair is lovely. If I had hair as beautiful as yours, I'd be twirling it all the time.

SHANNON
My hair's a mess. I know you're only being nice and everything, but no matter how much you like someone, there's always going to be something about them that annoys you. I had this boyfriend once, every time we came back from somewhere, he'd take his sneakers off and start to scratch the soles of his feet — it drove me crazy, not to mention…

SEAN
I don't have itchy feet, and if I did, I'd be sure to only scratch them in private.

SHANNON
That's because you're very considerate.

SEAN
I'd never do anything to offend you.

SHANNON
I wish I could say the same.

SEAN
I can't imagine you offending anyone.

SHANNON
Really? You must have noticed when we were at the movies and I, in my usually annoying manner, started talking and commenting on the action. I'm sure there were more than a few people in the audience who definitely didn't appreciate me prattling on, it's just that sometimes I can't stop myself…

SEAN
It didn't bother me. I'm always interested in everything you have to say.

SHANNON
Now come on, seriously, I know what I'm like — there must be some little peculiarity about me that irritates you, just a little bit.

SEAN
Nope, can't think of anything.

SHANNON
Yes, you can. You know I suck my thumb when I'm reading or concentrating on something — I've seen you look at me.

SEAN
I think it's sexy.

SHANNON
You're hopeless. Come on now, I insist. You have to think of one thing I do or say or something about me that you <u>don't</u> find adorable. OK? Just one tiny imperfection. I insist.

SEAN
You insist?

SHANNON
I insist. I absolutely insist.

SEAN
Well…

SHANNON
Ah, see, there is one thing. Come on, out with it.

SEAN
It's nothing really.

SHANNON
Come on, you have to say it. Humor me. I'm going to pry it out of you anyway, one way or another.

SEAN
It's such a small thing…

SHANNON
Remember, we're talking about <u>my</u> imperfections, not yours.

SEAN
My imperfections?

SHANNON
"It's such a small thing"?

SEAN
Sorry, I don't know what…

SHANNON
Never mind, never mind.

SEAN
Oh, "a small thing," oh, I get it, you're referring to…

SHANNON
No, no, no, come on now, I'm only kidding.

SEAN
I really love your sense of humor.

SHANNON
Sense of humor aside, come on. I'm waiting. Just one little thing that bugs you.

SEAN
Well, *(sigh)* alright then, I suppose if I had to pick something, I'd say it was your laugh.

SHANNON
My laugh?

SEAN
It's just a tiny bit… grating sometimes.

SHANNON
How is it grating?

SEAN
I don't know, you insisted on me saying something.

SHANNON
No, I don't understand. How do you mean?

ALMOST PERFECT

SEAN
(*nervously chewing on his fingernails*) It grates… sometimes.

SHANNON
My laugh?

SEAN
Other than that, I just adore everything about you.

SHANNON
Hang on a minute, you have to explain. My laugh? How does it grate?

SEAN
It just grates… a little bit.

SHANNON
No, go on, show me, you do my laugh, show me what you mean.

SEAN
You want me to laugh?

SHANNON
As me. Laugh like you think I do.

SEAN
I can't.

SHANNON
No, please, demonstrate. Please. It's okay.

SEAN
Really? Well, it's a bit like, you know…

> *SEAN does an impression of Shannon's laugh. It should be totally over-the-top, sounding something like a cross between a squealing pig and an angry donkey. Goes on for up to 30 seconds and needs to be extremely exaggerated for maximum comic effect.*

SHANNON
I see.

The mood has changed significantly.

SEAN
It's no big deal or anything. I can learn to live with it.

SHANNON
You can? *(sarcastic)* That's a relief.

SEAN
What about me, though? There must be hundreds of things about me that really wind you up. I mean, where do you start? I'm sure I must be one of the most irritating people you've ever met. But that's what's so amazing about you, that's why I like you so much, that you can put up with me in the first place.

SHANNON
I suppose there is one thing.

SEAN
Only one? Are you sure? You're telling me there's only one thing about me that annoys you?

SHANNON
Well, one thing in particular.

SEAN
You don't have to tell me. I know. I do come on a bit strong, I know, I'm the first to admit it. I can be a bit, you know, over-the-top.

SHANNON
Really, I hadn't noticed.

SEAN
(starts biting fingernails again) Is it my fingernails, me biting my fingernails?

SHANNON

There is that, I suppose.

SEAN

Oh, I know what it is, you don't have to tell me, I have this annoying habit of sticking my tongue out between my lips when…

SHANNON

It's not that.

SEAN

Is it my dust allergy?

SHANNON

No, I was thinking more about the way you eat.

SEAN

The way I eat?

SHANNON

Yes, the way you eat.

SEAN

How do I eat?

SHANNON

It's something like this…

> SHANNON *goes into an extended demonstration of exaggerated chewing, chomping, slurping, burping, and picking teeth with fingers, as gross as possible, again for maximum comic effect.*

SEAN

Oh, really, I hadn't realized.

SHANNON

No, I don't suppose you had.

SEAN
Well, we're none of us perfect, I suppose.

SHANNON
No.

SEAN
(resigned)
(*beat*) I'm guessing we're breaking up here.

SHANNON
Yes.

SEAN
I don't suppose there's any chance…

SHANNON
No.

SEAN
Can we maybe…

SHANNON
No.

SEAN
You want me to…

SHANNON
Yes.

SEAN *makes to leave*

SEAN
Would it make any difference if…

SHANNON
No.

ALMOST PERFECT

SEAN

I suppose I'd better just...

SHANNON

Yes.

SEAN leaves. SHANNON picks up her book, or a menu, and sticks her thumb in her mouth as she concentrates on the contents.

END OF PLAY

ARMCHAIR CRITIC

NICKY DENOVAN

Reprinted by permission of the author.

For performance rights, contact Nicky Denovan, nicky@nickydenovan.com

Synopsis
An award-winning theatre critic is summoned to his editor's office to explain his latest review. Could it be the end of the road? Can Clive keep his career on track? And who is really in the driver's seat?

Time
Present day

Characters
DAN, male, 30s, editor of a national British newspaper

CLIVE, male, 60s, award-winning theatre critic

Setting
Interior of newspaper editor DAN's office

Estimated run time
10 minutes

ARMCHAIR CRITIC

CLIVE is taking a seat across the desk from DAN.

DAN
Thanks for coming in, Clive.

CLIVE
Not a problem. I so rarely get into the office these days. It's nice to drink someone else's coffee for a change. Although frankly, this is pretty terrible.

DAN
Yep. We've had to cut costs in the newsroom. The night team have been bringing in their own loo roll for over a year.

CLIVE
Have they really? Gosh. Different times. I remember when it was all ciggies smoldering in the ashtray, bashing away at stories on rickety typewriters, and all the Garibaldis you could eat. You're too young to remember, of course.

DAN
Times have certainly changed. Look, Clive, it's rather a difficult matter.

CLIVE
Oh?

DAN
I've had a complaint.

CLIVE
A complaint?

DAN
Letter to the editor. About your latest review.

CLIVE
What, the Pinter?

DAN

Yes. The Pinter.

CLIVE

I see. So… disgruntled director? Lead actor with a fatally wounded ego? I can only judge exactly what I see on the stage. That's always been my guiding principle.

DAN

No. Nobody from the production. It's from a reader. And fellow theatre-goer.

CLIVE

Right.

DAN

They have an issue with the final paragraph of your piece.

CLIVE

You'll have to refresh my memory.

DAN

I've got it here.

CLIVE

Two reviews a week for twenty years, and they all tend to blend into one another.

DAN
(reading)

"As this problematic production lumbered towards its iconic climactic scene, the audience was left desperately searching for a reason to care and, audibly, its tickets for the cloakroom. When the curtain mercifully lowered on the play's final line, it was a lackluster conclusion, entirely in keeping with a piece that was terminally lacking in energy, impact, and emotional depth."

CLIVE

Well, it's… robust. Might be a touch on the harsh side. But I think you'll find it's broadly fair.

DAN

Possibly. Except it didn't happen.

CLIVE

Sorry?

DAN

It didn't happen. The closing moments you describe here didn't happen.

CLIVE

What do you mean?

DAN

You really need me to tell you?

CLIVE

I wish you would.

DAN

What happened, Clive, is that, just before the final scene, the leading man started extravagantly vomiting thanks to a dodgy pizza, the understudy got accidentally stuck in the dressing room toilet and couldn't go on, someone backstage set off the venue's fire alarm making a cheese toastie, and the entire show had to be abandoned in chaos. The reader calls it — what was the phrase? — "total and utter carnage."

CLIVE

What? But that's not right. They must be talking about a different performance. Matinee, maybe?

DAN

No, there was no matinee that day, and you specifically note the date. (*pointing*) Here. And your filed expenses include a train ticket stamped with the same date. (*pointing*) There. Plus, I checked the reader's account of events with the venue.

CLIVE

And?

DAN
They confirmed it.

CLIVE
I don't know what to tell you.

DAN
So you, award-winning theatre critic and Chief Theatrical Correspondent for this newspaper, saw the same play on the same night as our valued reader here, but you didn't think it worth mentioning in your review that the evening had collapsed like a clown car, ending in complete farce?

CLIVE
I'm sorry. I just can't explain it. I wrote what I saw.

DAN
Clive.

CLIVE
Yes?

DAN
You weren't there, were you?

CLIVE
Excuse me?

DAN
You weren't at the theatre that night.

CLIVE
What are you talking about?

DAN
I did some digging. Asked around a bit… Nobody has ever seen you at the theatre… Any theatre.

CLIVE
Well, that's ridiculous.

DAN
Oh, there are always rumors that you're going to be "in" on a particular night, and a frisson of nervous excitement runs through the assembled company, but nobody has ever actually laid eyes on you. It seems you're the Scarlet Pimpernel of the West End.

CLIVE
I like to be discreet. Sneak in as the lights go down, shuffle out during final bows. That sort of thing.

DAN
Is that right? It just so happens that the box office for the Pinter recently had a CCTV system installed.

CLIVE
Oh. Did they?

DAN
Yes, they did. They've had a spate of ticket thefts and wanted to get to the bottom of it. So, I rang the theatre manager and asked them to spool through the images from that night.

CLIVE
Crikey, this is all getting a bit dramatic, isn't it? I wish I hadn't had that coffee now. It would make a better play than the Pinter, actually. Go on.

DAN
You're nowhere to be seen in the footage from that evening. But someone did collect the tickets in your name.

CLIVE
Are you going to tell me who?

DAN
No. You are.
(*producing image*) Do you recognize this woman?

CLIVE
It's a bit blurry. I couldn't say for definite.

DAN
Take your time.

CLIVE
You're not going to bring in a lineup, are you? Only I've left my distance glasses at home.

DAN
Enough, Clive. Straight answer. Did you or did you not attend the Pinter that night?

CLIVE
Just to be clear, we're talking about Harold Pinter, aren't we?

DAN
Straight. Answer.

CLIVE
No.

DAN
Right. And have you actually graced with your presence any of the theatrical productions to which this newspaper has provided complimentary tickets and generous reimbursement of your expenses over a period of twenty years?

CLIVE
No.

DAN
I see.

CLIVE
Actually, that's unfair. I definitely saw a couple way back. I'm thinking "Carousel" but I couldn't tell you the year.

DAN
Help me out here, Clive, because I am struggling with this. How on earth have you managed to pursue a successful career as a professional theatre critic on a national newspaper for nigh on two decades, without setting foot inside a theatre?

CLIVE
I've been dreading this. But I knew it. I knew this day would come. All right. Let me explain.

DAN
I'd love it if you could.

CLIVE
I've been sending… (*pause*)

DAN
Sending in your best guess based on that day's horoscope?

CLIVE
No. I've been sending… (*pause*)

DAN
Sending out psychic signals to the audience and beaming their thoughts back in via the medium of telepathy?

CLIVE
I've been sending… a stand-in.

DAN
A stand-in?

CLIVE
Well, a sit-in. My mother likes to take her own cushion.

DAN
Your mother?

CLIVE
She's very sprightly for a 94-year-old. Absolutely adores the theatre. She was over the moon when I got given this job. She goes with a friend. They make a real night of it. Pre-theatre dinner at The Wiltshire, glad rags on, cocktails, the whole shebang. She rings me up after each show, tells me what she liked and disliked about the production, gives me a rundown of the performances, the set, any particular points of interest. I jot it all down, and then I put my own distinctive spin on it.

DAN
Spin's the right word. A web of deceit is what you've been spinning. I just don't understand.

CLIVE
Well, she must have left the theatre early for some reason and entirely missed the last scene. I'll be having words with her.

DAN
I mean, I don't understand this. Why the deception?

CLIVE
I had no choice. I had to protect my secret.

DAN
What secret?

CLIVE
It's… embarrassing.

DAN
Embarrassment is the least of our problems right now.

CLIVE
Some years ago, I developed a fear of travelling. I'm not talking about being a bit cheesed off with the daily commute. I'm talking sheer panic, crippling terror at the thought of getting into a vehicle. It didn't matter whether it was a plane or a pedalo. Just the idea of getting on a bus or on a train or into a car… the very prospect was enough to send me into a spiral of dread. Sweating, palpitations, a feeling of crushing, imminent doom.

DAN
But you were the Travel Correspondent for four years.

CLIVE
Yes, that was very, very inconvenient.

DAN
Don't tell me you sent your mother on those trips.

CLIVE
Of course, I didn't send my mother.

DAN
Thank goodness for that.

CLIVE
I sent my brother-in-law.

DAN
Oh, for God's sake.

CLIVE
He was only too happy to do it. He bought a Jet Ski with the air miles.

DAN
I can't believe I'm hearing this. So if all this is true, how did you get to the office today?

CLIVE
Two Valium and a "breathe through the stress" instrumental track on loop.

Gesturing towards his ears

Earpieces.

DAN
I thought those were your hearing aids. You claimed them on expenses.

CLIVE
Yes. Sorry about that.

DAN
What about therapy?

CLIVE
I've tried everything. I've even been hypnotized. Nothing works.

DAN
So, what do we do now?

CLIVE
How do you mean?

DAN
We can't just carry on sending your mother on a jolly to the theatre twice a week with you writing the reviews second-hand. It's fraudulent.

CLIVE
Well. Why not? If it isn't broken…

DAN
It is a bit broken, Clive.

CLIVE

I'm an award-winning critic. I've given this paper influence. Clout. My verdict — if it's a good one — is plastered on every poster on every billboard across this city. I can make or break a production. Mine is the opinion that people want to read.

DAN

Your mother's opinion is what they actually read.

CLIVE

She's my eyes and ears. My special envoy. But I'm the writer. I'm the talent.

DAN

Are you serious?

CLIVE

Perfectly. Listen. What's the problem? You get the services of the best and most loved theatre writer this country has to offer. Not my words — The Ollie Awards 2003. And my mother gets to toddle up to town two nights a week, sit in the best seats in the house with a dear old pal, eating her own weight in luxury ice cream. Did I tell you about the slap-up meal at The Wiltshire?

DAN

You did mention it.

CLIVE

Well, that comes out of my pocket. Honestly, she's having the time of her life.

DAN

I'm sorry. None of this is right. You know we're going to have to sort this out, don't you?

CLIVE

So what are you going to do? Fire me? You've already said times are tough. Circulation's down. Revenue's down. Competition is up. Costs are sky-high. So what... you're going to sack me and hand our loyal readers a ready-made excuse to buy a rival newspaper, are you?

DAN

I have a duty to be straight with them.

CLIVE

You have a duty to deliver what they want. And what they want is my theatre column. Twice a week. Have you got this week's online readership figures?

DAN

You know it's our most-read section.

CLIVE

Of course, it is. You want to go to the owner of the paper and tell her you've lost your star critic? Well, go on then. Be my guest. Ring her up.

DAN

Just give me a minute.

CLIVE

Take your time.

DAN

What does your mother say about all this? She knows what's going on? And she's fine with it?

CLIVE

I'll call her if you don't believe me.

CLIVE grabs the desk phone and dials his mother.

Mother? It's me. I'm in the office. Don't worry about that. They've rumbled us. Yep. Uh-huh. Well, you didn't tell me that you left the play early last week. Well, you did. You missed a great big chunk of action. The Pinter.

(*shouting*) The Pinter. Right… Right… Right.

CLIVE covers the phone mouthpiece and addresses DAN.

She says the play was dreadful. So dull she and her mate nodded off. Next thing she knew, she was being woken up in the auditorium by the theatre staff rustling bin bags. She must have snored through the entire debacle.

Listening to his mother again

All right. I'll ask him. Hang on.

(*to DAN*) She wants to speak to you.

DAN
Okay. Er… (*to CLIVE*) What's her name?

CLIVE
Jean. Jean Watts.

DAN
Hello. Yes. Yes, I am. That's right. Yes. Yes, he is. Yes, I know. Oh, I'm glad. Yes. Kind of you to say. Right. Um… let me think about it. I'll let you know. Okay. I will. Thank you. Goodbye, Mrs. Watts. Goodbye.

CLIVE
Well?

DAN
She's quite a character.

CLIVE
That's one way of putting it.

DAN
She said I was doing a very good job.

CLIVE
She gets the paper every day. Never misses.

DAN
She says you're a good son. Very thoughtful.

CLIVE
One does one's best.

DAN
And she thinks I should give you a pay rise.

CLIVE
Always been a wise woman, my mother. Well, looks like we've both had a five-star review there. So… How about it?

END OF PLAY

CAN YOU HEAR ME NOW?

MOREY NORKIN

Reprinted by permission of the author.
For performance rights, contact Morey Norkin, mnorkin@hotmail.com

Synopsis
Bell and Watson invent a way to revolutionize communication. If only they can find enough string.

Time
March 10, 1876, or anytime in an alternate universe

Characters
BELL, any gender, any age, any race, scientist, enthusiastic

WATSON, any gender, any age, any race, scientist, skeptical

Setting
A lab, sometime in the past. Historical accuracy in setting or casting is not necessary. Two tables are provided, one for each scientist. They are covered with scientific equipment, books, etc.

Estimated run time
8 minutes

CAN YOU HEAR ME NOW?

BELL and WATSON each wear white lab coats and stand behind separate lab tables. WATSON's table has various glasses and beakers. BELL's table has books or boxes, or anything to obscure the view of the work in progress.

BELL
Eureka! Watson, come quickly! I need you!

WATSON
(startled)

Do you have to shout? What have you discovered this time, Dr. Bell? A longer-lasting chewing gum? My sense of taste still hasn't recovered from the last one.

BELL
This is life-changing! This will revolutionize communication!

WATSON
Well, let's see it!

BELL
Slowly produces two paper cups connected by a string.

Voila!

WATSON
It looks like two paper cups connected by a string.

BELL
Exactly!

WATSON
Exactly what does it do?

BELL
I call it a "tell-a-cup." You tell another person something into one cup, and they hear it through the other cup.

WATSON
Amazing!

BELL

Yes! And here's the truly revolutionary part. The other person can respond through the other cup! Thus, establishing bi-directional communication!

WATSON

Amazing! May I try it?

BELL

I insist!

> *BELL hands a cup to WATSON. They move apart but are separated by no more than a few feet.*

BELL

Now, hold the cup up to your ear.

> *WATSON uses the wrong end.*

BELL

Not like that! Put the open end against your ear!

WATSON

Perhaps we will need to include instructions.

BELL

Yes. Make a note of that, will you?

> *WATSON starts to move to the table, but the string won't stretch that far. WATSON is a little confused as to what to do.*
>
> *BELL takes the cup from WATSON.*
>
> *WATSON proceeds to the table and writes something, and then returns. WATSON takes the cup and again holds it the wrong way.*
>
> *BELL turns the cup around and presses it to WATSON's ear.*

BELL

Ready?

WATSON

Ready!

BELL

Speaking loudly into the cup.

Hello, Watson!

WATSON

Speaking loudly but not into the cup.

Hello, Dr. Bell!

BELL

You're supposed to speak into the cup!

WATSON

But I hear you just fine without it.

BELL

Let's try this again.

Stage whisper.

Watson, come quickly! I need you!

WATSON

No response.

BELL

Watson, come quickly! I need you!

WATSON
No response.

BELL
(shouting)
Watson, come quickly! I need you!

WATSON
You don't need to shout! I heard you the first time.

BELL
Then why didn't you say something?!

WATSON
I was already here.

BELL
But you heard me? Through the cup?

WATSON
Clear as a bell. (*giggling*) Oh my. Clear as a bell. (*laughing*) Bell… bell. Do you see?

BELL
Yes, I see. Enjoy your little joke. But the tell-a-cup is no laughing matter. This will change society in ways like nothing before.

WATSON
That may be true, Dr. Bell. But I feel obliged to mention a few possible design flaws that we may need to address.

BELL
Flaws?! What flaws?!

WATSON
Well, first of all, the string. It's too short.

BELL

I can make it longer. Next?

WATSON

I still have a problem with the string. Even if you make it longer, we can only talk on the tell-a-cup when we are together. In which case, we can just talk as we are doing now.

BELL

Watson, you present a good argument. What I believe we can glean from your remarks is that we need to be able to communicate with our cups over long distances.

WATSON

Something like that.

BELL

That would take a lot of string.

WATSON

Forget the string! I'm sorry. There's also the cups.

BELL

What's wrong with the cups?

WATSON squeezes the cup and crushes it.

BELL

Right. So we need a stronger cup.

WATSON

Also, how does one distinguish one cup from another?

BELL

I'm not sure I follow you…

WATSON
Let's say you have a cup, I have a cup, and your mother has a cup.

BELL
My mother? She has no understanding of technology!

WATSON
Fine. Your father, then.

BELL
Not much difference, but go on.

WATSON
If you want to talk to your father, how do you contact his cup and not mine?

BELL
I suppose I would visit him at home and we would then talk by tell-a-cup.

WATSON
Which brings us back to the original problem with the string.

BELL
I think I'm beginning to understand. We need a device that is sturdy yet compact enough to be held in the palm of one's hand, allowing communication over great distances without the use of strings. A stringless tell-a-cup!

WATSON
Brilliant! Let me write this down.

WATSON goes to the table and makes some notes.

BELL
But we still need some way to distinguish one device from another.

WATSON
Something unique. Like a number.

CAN YOU HEAR ME NOW?

BELL

Yes! A tell-a-cup number! I think I should be number one and you should be number two, if you don't mind.

WATSON

I wouldn't have it any other way.

BELL

So, that's settled. Anything else?

WATSON

What if we add a typewriter?

BELL

A typewriter? On top of a tell-a-cup? How could you possibly hold that in your hand?

WATSON

I'm just brainstorming. But what if we could somehow make a typewriter small enough to fit on the tell-a-cup? It might be possible to not only communicate using speech but also through written messages!

BELL

We have the post office for that.

WATSON

Yes, I know. But that can take so much time. Imagine if you try to connect with someone on the tell-a-cup but for some reason, they don't respond. If your message is truly important, you send a written note instead that is available at the recipient's convenience.

BELL

Interesting. I use all my fingers to type. How could we possibly make a typewriter small enough?

WATSON

Hmmm... What if you only type with your thumbs?

BELL

My thumbs… Yes! Our thumbs distinguish humankind from the rest of the animal kingdom!

BELL does some exaggerated thumb movements as if using a smartphone.

Ow! Well, I'm sure that won't be a problem. This is extraordinary! Our humble tell-a-cup has now become a device that every man, woman, and child will clamor for. People spending countless hours sharing information with family and friends at the exact moment that life's events are occurring!

A realization.

BELL

They won't want to do much of anything else. Waiting for that instant response. Sharing the most mundane information. Perhaps even making up fanciful stories because real life is so dull or terrifying. All face-to-face communication will cease. We will lose our humanity.

WATSON

We could make a fortune!

BELL

Once again, Watson, you make a compelling argument. What if, in addition to a typewriter, we also add a camera…?

Blackout.

END OF PLAY

CHEMISTRY DATE

LENNY HORT

from *Forces of Nature*

Synopsis
Dating show host Iona Bond tries to find the chemistry between Chlorine and Sodium.

Time
The present

Characters
IONA BOND, female, any age, glamorous dating show host.

CHLORINE, female, any age. Perhaps she has yellow-green hair and clothing.

SODIUM, male, any age. Perhaps wears a shiny, silvery-white metallic suit. He and CHLORINE should be similar in age but different in race or ethnicity.

Setting
A romantic seaside resort

Estimated run time
7-8 minutes

CHEMISTRY DATE

IONA BOND, a glamorous TV host, appears.

IONA

She's been described as the ultimate clean freak. He's a bit of a softy, yet his personality is positively explosive. Friends say she's a gas to hang out with, but watch out for caustic remarks. He's got a lonesome electron that he's eager to share, but the way this boy reacts, you'll need to handle him with gloves and safety goggles. Did I mention that both of them are deadly poisons? I'm Iona Bond, and you're watching "Chemistry Date," the show that brings lonely elements together in search of their own chemical romance. Today, we're at this romantic seaside resort to introduce Sodium and Chlorine. How will these two react to each other? Will Atom find his Eve?

CHLORINE enters and looks warily about her.

And it looks like the lovely Chlorine is the first to arrive for a seaside rendezvous.

CHLORINE

Okay, Iona, where's this Bozium you're trying to fix me up with?

IONA

His name is Sodium, and I think you two were made for each other.

CHLORINE

You said that about Helium. Kind of a lightweight, don't you think, and totally inert.

IONA

That was different.

CHLORINE

And Hydrogen. That still burns.

IONA

Enough with the acid remarks, Chlorine. Here comes our boy.

CHLORINE

Swell.

IONA
Give him a chance.

SODIUM enters with a gift bag.

SODIUM
Ms. Bond. Sorry, I'm late.

IONA
Don't worry about it. There's someone I'd like you to meet.

SODIUM
You must be —

CHLORINE
Chlorine.

SODIUM
Sodium. Chemical symbol N-A from the Latin natrium.

CHLORINE
C-L.

IONA
Is there anything I can do to stir things up for the two of you?

CHLORINE
The last thing we need is a catalyst.

IONA
As long as you're both feeling in your element, I'll leave you to it.

IONA withdraws.

CHLORINE
So.

CHEMISTRY DATE

SODIUM
Sodium.

CHLORINE
Yeah, I got that.

SODIUM
Number 11 on the Periodic Table.

CHLORINE
Isn't it kind of soon to be exchanging numbers?

SODIUM
Sorry. I — I brought you a little something I made.

He hands CHLORINE the gift bag.

CHLORINE
How sweet. It's —

SODIUM
A sodium vapor lamp. Not great for color, but very efficient. Mostly for outdoor lighting, I guess.

CHLORINE
And you make these.

SODIUM
With plenty of help from Mercury and Aluminum. I shouldn't take all the credit.

CHLORINE
Aluminum, huh? Al and I worked together on creating aluminum chlorohydrate.

SODIUM
Isn't that the main ingredient in deodorant?

CHLORINE
You got it.

SODIUM
Impressive.

CHLORINE
Afraid I didn't bring you anything.

SODIUM
That's all right.

CHLORINE
I mean, what would you think if I just met you and the first thing I did was hand you a stick of deodorant?

SODIUM
I wouldn't make a big stink about it. I've heard nice things about you.

CHLORINE
Oh?

SODIUM
Ms. Bond says you're very big in the cleaning business.

CHLORINE
Well, yes, that's true. I bleach clothes, I disinfect floors, I even have a sideline cleaning pools.

SODIUM
Remarkable.

CHLORINE
I understand this place has a very nice pool if you want to check it out.

SODIUM
Probably not a good idea. Truth is, I don't mix well with water.

CHLORINE
But isn't that you in club soda?

SODIUM
In the form of sodium bicarbonate, yes. But in my pure form, not a good idea. Drop me in water and I catch fire and explode.

CHLORINE
Wait — that was you in that video on YouTube?

SODIUM
That was me.

CHLORINE
O-M-G. I never would have figured you for the daredevil type. You seem so…

SODIUM
Nerdy?

CHLORINE
In a good way.

SODIUM
I'm full of surprises. But it's no secret that I'm not very stable.

CHLORINE
I think you're sweet.

SODIUM
Nobody's ever called me that before.

CHLORINE
You are. And I've really enjoyed meeting you.

SODIUM
Likewise.

CHLORINE
But the two of us — we're so different. I wouldn't want you to think I'm racist or anything, but me a gas and you a solid…

SODIUM
A solid who doesn't mix well with liquids.

CHLORINE
So maybe it's time we called off Iona's little experiment and said good night.

SODIUM
Good night, then.

CHLORINE
Good night. I'll remember you.

SODIUM
And I most certainly will remember you.

SODIUM extends his hand, and CHLORINE takes it. There is a sudden change.

CHLORINE
Oh.

SODIUM
Oh my.

CHLORINE
Don't go.

SODIUM
No way.

CHLORINE
Are you feeling —

CHEMISTRY DATE

SODIUM

I'm feeling —

SODIUM AND CHLORINE
(simultaneously)

Chemistry!

THEY join in a seemingly endless embrace. IONA appears and pulls a shade or curtain in front of SODIUM and CHLORINE.

IONA

Let's give these lovebirds some privacy, shall we? It seems our little experiment has been a success after all. And so Chlorine and Sodium have bonded ionically as Sodium Chloride. More commonly known as Salt. It's crystal clear that these two are a match made in chemistry heaven. Let's check in on the happy compound.

IONA reveals SODIUM and CHLORINE, all in white, holding hands or locking arms.

You two look positively perfect together.

SODIUM AND CHLORINE
(simultaneously)

We are one now.

SODIUM

She's the yin to my yang.

CHLORINE
(Showing IONA her ring finger)

Did you see the electron he gave me?

IONA

Priceless.

SODIUM

I could just tell there was an empty spot in that outermost shell of yours.

CHLORINE
You always say the sweetest — I mean the saltiest things.

SODIUM
And thanks to you, darling, I don't have any more blow-ups when I go in the water.

CHLORINE
You can always find us in the ocean. Or the Great Salt Lake.

SODIUM
Care to go for a dip?

CHLORINE
The very thought, and I practically dissolve into tears of joy.

IONA
See you guys at the dinner table.

SODIUM and CHLORINE exit together. IONA addresses the audience.

IONA
So there you have it. Two deadly substances when we first met them. But with the right chemistry, they've become essential to life on Earth as we know it. Join us next week when we'll try introducing Oxygen to the Hydrogen twins. Water the chances that things will get wet and wild? I'm Iona Bond. See you next time on "Chemistry Date"!

END OF PLAY

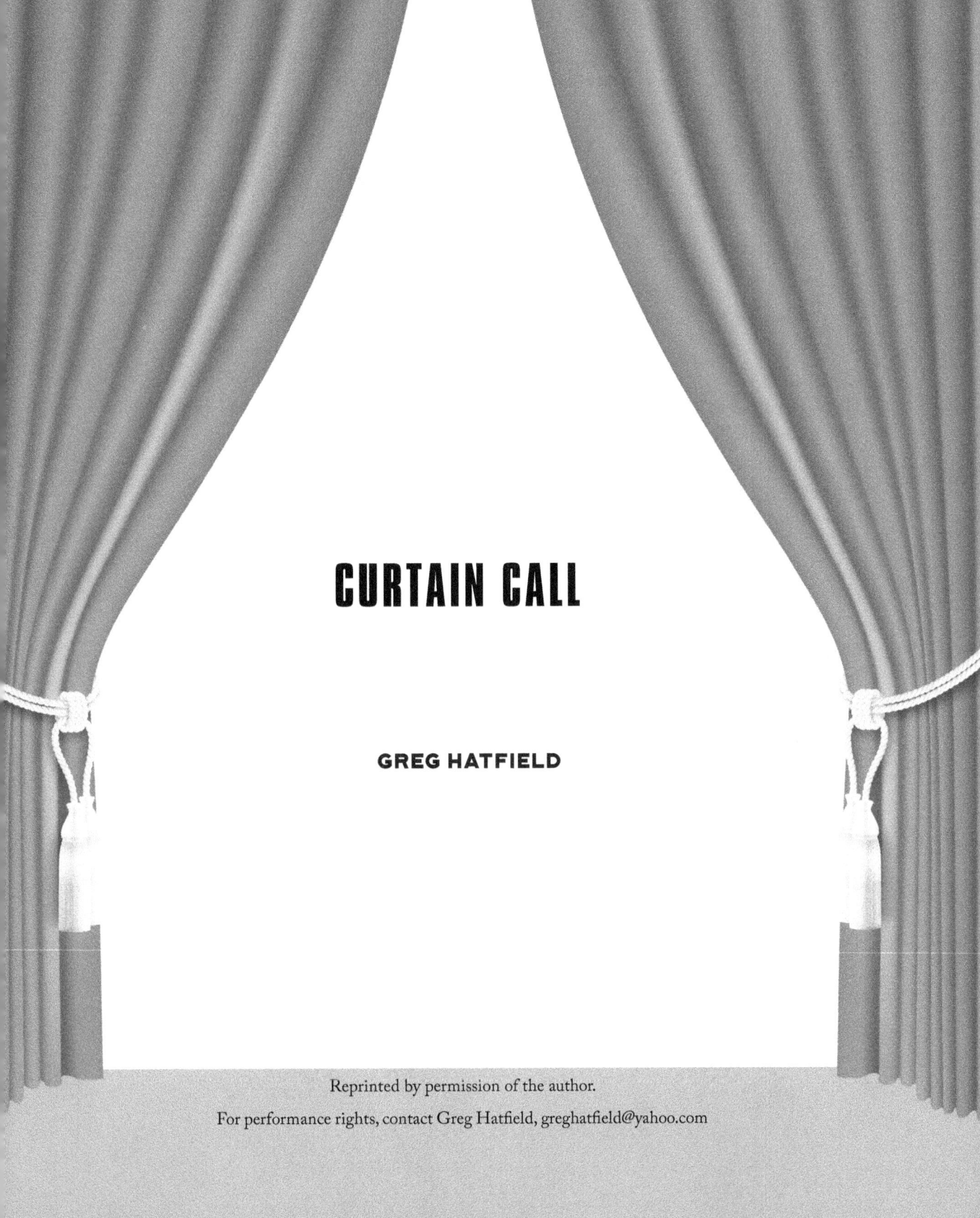

CURTAIN CALL

GREG HATFIELD

Reprinted by permission of the author.
For performance rights, contact Greg Hatfield, greghatfield@yahoo.com

Synopsis
The play is a hit, but the two stars of Broadway don't feel it's working, and their performances aren't up to their usual standards, so they want out.

Time
1938

Characters
LYDIA FRANCIS, female, 40ish, but will happily shave a decade off her age. One of the most acclaimed actresses of her time.

ALLEN HART, male, late 40s. One of the most acclaimed actors of his time, a perfectionist. Married to Lydia.

NEIL COLLINS, male, a boyish 40. Playwright, actor, successful. Best friends with the Harts, but in over his head with them on stage.

MARCIA McLEAN, female, 40-50. A celebrated actress in New York, who is Lydia's rival for the best parts on Broadway.

Setting
Broadway (NYC), backstage in the Harts' dressing room on opening night.

Estimated run time
12 minutes

CURTAIN CALL

Backstage at the end of a play. Offstage, we hear the audience thunderously applauding and cheering. The applause does not stop; it is a standing ovation. LYDIA FRANCIS enters, slightly bowing to the audience and half-smiling as she enters the room. She is wearing a period dress, perhaps Elizabethan. Once she is inside, she wearily sits in a chair and sinks her head into her hands. The applause doesn't stop. ALLEN HART enters, bowing slightly to the audience and half-smiling as he enters the room. He is wearing a period costume too, perhaps a powdered wig and fake eyebrows. Once he is inside, he sits wearily in a chair, takes the wig off his head, removes his eyebrows, and sinks his head into his hands.

The applause doesn't stop.

NEIL COLLINS enters, bowing deeply and with a great smile and waving, acknowledging the entire audience as he enters the room. He is wearing something military, perhaps. He is all smiles and blowing kisses to the audience, obviously triumphant.

NEIL
(to the audience)

Thank you! Thank you! We love you!

NEIL is full of energy, pacing as he can't stay still, as he says to LYDIA and ALLEN.

My God! That was exhilarating. What a night! Never have I had an opening night like this. "The Spoken Word" is a hit, my friends, and I wrote it. And acted in it wonderfully, I might add. This will go down in history as one of the best opening nights in theatre! I've never seen anything like it.

He now notices LYDIA and ALLEN in their despair.

What are you two doing? You look like lumps.

LYDIA

Isn't it obvious?

NEIL

If it were obvious, I wouldn't have asked.

ALLEN
Read the room, Neil.

NEIL
Read the room? We just had the best opening night ever, and you two are acting like we just killed your puppy. What is wrong with you?

LYDIA
I think it best you sit down.

NEIL
I'm not sitting down. I'm too wound up to sit. But you'd better tell me.

ALLEN
We're leaving the play.

NEIL
What! You've got to be kidding. What brought this on?

LYDIA
I would think it rather clear, Neil.

NEIL
Well, it's not. I want an explanation.

ALLEN
You heard the audience. We heard the audience. We can tell.

NEIL
Tell what? This is getting ridiculous.

LYDIA
The truth of the matter is, Neil…

ALLEN
We weren't particularly good. We can bring nothing to the play.

NEIL
What?! Are you both crazy? You were magnificent. The Magnificent Harts strike again. It will be the talk of the town.

LYDIA
Please, Neil. Don't try to wish away the pain. We know we weren't good.

ALLEN
Don't embarrass us with praise we don't deserve.

NEIL
Where is this coming from? Did you hear the ovation tonight? Thirteen curtain calls. Thirteen! Do you ever hear of audiences giving thirteen "pity" curtain calls?

ALLEN
They're just being polite.

NEIL
What on earth makes you think you were bad?

LYDIA
It started in Act One.

ALLEN
Scene Five.

NEIL
The lunch scene.

LYDIA
Yes. Allen placed the glass on the wrong side of the serving tray.

ALLEN
I don't know what got into me. A total lack of concentration, I suppose.

LYDIA
That concerned me.

NEIL
Oh, it concerned you, did it?

LYDIA
Yes. I saw it right away. Of course, I looked at Allen and saw the terror in his eyes. That threw me. I panicked as well, and before I knew it, my head was moving back and forth as I delivered the lines. *(She demonstrates.)*

NEIL
Back and forth?

LYDIA
Ever so slightly.

ALLEN
But it threw me off. I nearly forgot to serve the finger sandwiches at the proper time.

NEIL
I don't know how you ever recovered.

ALLEN
I didn't. I was thinking about it for the rest of the play.

LYDIA
He was off, alright. As a matter of fact, Allen, your scene in Act Three wasn't especially good.

ALLEN
The confession scene?

LYDIA
Yes. It was stodgy, I thought. You usually say those lines with zip and energy, and tonight, nothing.

NEIL
Now, wait a minute. I'm in that scene with Allen. I didn't notice anything wrong.

ALLEN
Well, you wouldn't, Neil. That's something only actors notice.

NEIL
The audience loved it. We got laugh after laugh in that scene.

LYDIA
(gently)
They don't know any better, Neil.

ALLEN
And what about you, Lydia? In Act Two, Scene Four.

LYDIA
Oh, you're bringing that up.

ALLEN
Do you think I was the only one who noticed?

NEIL
What the hell was wrong with that scene?

LYDIA
I think Allen was referring to the fact that I totally misplayed the character for at least three pages of dialogue.

ALLEN
And the "hand gesture" thing.

LYDIA does the hand gesture thing, flaunting it in front of ALLEN's face.

LYDIA
(defiantly)
There it is for all to see!

ALLEN
You've never been good in comedies, Lydia. Perhaps the critics are right. You are hobbled by your abilities.

LYDIA

How dare you, Mr. Costume-Drama-Only Actor! If it weren't for me, you would never have done a comedy in your life. I was the reason we were cast together in "Earnest"! They wanted me, but I said, "Oh, I couldn't do it without Allen."

ALLEN

I carried that show! You were a mess right up until curtain. I had to reassure you time and time again.

LYDIA

Only because I was trying to fix every scene we were in!

NEIL
(pleading)

What is going on here? Again, Lydia, the scene we played was letter-perfect. You are a marvelous comedy actor. Trust me, the scene was wonderful.

LYDIA

Maybe if I had had extra rehearsal time, I could have overcome it.

ALLEN

We could have had rehearsal from now till Doomsday, and it wouldn't have mattered.

LYDIA

I will never act with you again! We are finished.

NEIL

I am going crazy with you two. There was nothing wrong with the play. Nothing! It was a smash. Why would you fool with my mind like this? You know I need a hit. My entire career is on the line.

ALLEN

We're as disappointed as you are, I'm sure. You put a lot of work into it, I know, and we're sorry we couldn't deliver. It must make you so upset.

NEIL

I'm not upset! *(shouting)* I'm happy! Happy, I tell you! We have a hit. We'll play the entire season to sellout audiences.

LYDIA

Well, let's not get too hasty. I'm sure the reviews will be a letdown.

ALLEN

They'll see right through us.

NEIL
(sternly)

You both are out of your minds. This play is solid. Nothing is wrong with the play or your acting.

Just then MARCIA McLEAN enters.

LYDIA

Marcia! What a pleasant surprise. How lovely to see you.

LYDIA rises to kiss MARCIA on both cheeks.

ALLEN

Hello, Marcia.

He kisses her as well.

NEIL

Hello, Marcia. What did you think?

MARCIA
(ignoring NEIL)

Oh, Lydia, Allen. I came as soon as I could get backstage. It's quite crowded. Everyone's asking for you.

ALLEN

Were you at the performance?

MARCIA
Yes, Allen. I'm so sorry for you both. I know how you must feel.

NEIL
What are you talking about?

MARCIA
Oh, Neil. How devastated you must be.

She clasps NEIL's hands in hers.

NEIL
Not you, too?

LYDIA
How bad was it from the house?

MARCIA
Let's just say it was disappointing for some of us.

LYDIA (to ALLEN)
This is your fault.

ALLEN (to LYDIA)
You're the one who ruined the scene in the solarium.

LYDIA
How? I was perfect in that scene. You're the one who tried to step on my line about the clouds.

NEIL
That was part of the scene!

LYDIA
And your makeup was hideous. I've never seen eyebrows like that in all my years in the theatre.

NEIL

They're supposed to be hideous! *(to MARCIA)* See what you've done?

MARCIA

Don't shoot the messenger, Neil. I can't help it if they can't reasonably act.

NEIL
(to MARCIA, sternly)

Get out! I'm done talking about this.

(to LYDIA and ALLEN)

We've got a hit play, which I wrote, that will run for a long time. You two have a contract that stipulates you will be in it for the run of the play, and I swear upon the mighty hand of God that I will hold you to it, friends or no friends!

MARCIA (to LYDIA)

I'll call you once you've had time to mourn.

NEIL
(to MARCIA)

Now, if you would be so kind as to get the hell out of my theatre. And Marcia?

MARCIA

Yes, Neil?

NEIL
(sweetly)

I loved you in "Somerset." Quite a lovely performance.

MARCIA

Thank you, dear. I hope you find some solace in the days ahead.

She exits. LYDIA and ALLEN sit silently. NEIL paces.

NEIL
You two are really trying my patience. For years, all I've heard is, "Neil, please write a play for the three of us. Wouldn't it be fun if all of us were in a play together?" And what did I do? I wrote a play that all of us could do. Together. Because we're best friends. I'm ashamed of both of you. The biggest night of my life — the opening night of a play that I consider one of my best — sharing it with my dear, dear friends. And this is how I'm rewarded for my efforts. *(pause)* Well, leave the show if you must. I'll have the understudies do the part tomorrow night.

LYDIA
(sheepishly)

Well…

ALLEN
(bowing his head)

Maybe we were a little hasty.

LYDIA
Allen wasn't quite so bad in Scene Five. As a matter of fact, it was all I could do not to laugh myself.

ALLEN
And Lydia was marvelous in Scene Four. I have never seen such perfection.

LYDIA and ALLEN embrace.

LYDIA
I've always loved playing with you, Allen. There's no one else.

ALLEN
And you're wonderful in comedies, my love. I loved the hand gesture. It added so much.

They kiss tenderly.

NEIL
Finally. *(breathing heavily)* I may have a heart attack. Now, can we go out and enjoy the cast party on stage?

CURTAIN CALL

LYDIA
Of course, dear one. *(LYDIA kisses NEIL's cheek.)* It's a wonderful play. You're a marvelous writer. And you were absolutely perfect in the play, too.

ALLEN
(embracing NEIL)

Thank you for writing it for us. I enjoy playing the part with you and Lydia. You're as accomplished an actor as you are a writer.

NEIL
(shaking his head)

I swear I will never write another play for you two. Never! Not for a million dollars or any amount! And I was really good, wasn't I?

They head to the exit.

ALLEN
(stopping before they exit, to LYDIA)

You really didn't like my eyebrows, huh?

END OF PLAY

DRUMMER BOY

LISA DELLAGIARINO FERIEND

Reprinted by permission of the author.
For performance rights, contact Lisa Dellagiarino Feriend, lisadee1218@yahoo.com

Synopsis
The Little Drummer Boy shows up to worship the newborn king in Bethlehem, and it doesn't go great.

Time
The year 0 CE

Characters
MARY, female, in her teens, new mother, tired

JOSEPH, male, 20s, new father, tired

BOY, male, child, owns a drum, poor

Setting
A barn in Bethlehem in late December

Estimated run time
7 minutes

DRUMMER BOY

MARY sets baby Jesus in the manger as JOSEPH looks on.

MARY
He's finally asleep.

JOSEPH
Oh, good.

MARY
I'm exhausted.

JOSEPH
Maybe we can get a nap in before he wakes up.

They get comfortable as the Little Drummer BOY enters.

BOY
Excuse me?

JOSEPH
Shoot.

BOY
Is this the newborn king?

MARY
First, the shepherds, now a street urchin.

JOSEPH
Why did the angels have to scream our business to everyone?

MARY
I'll get rid of him.

(To the BOY) Hello, little boy. This is the newborn king. But he's finally asleep after screaming for just hours and hours, so if you want to hold him or something, can you come back later?

BOY
Oh, I don't need to hold him. I've just come to give him a gift.

JOSEPH
That's wonderful. Maybe come back —

BOY
But I'm a poor boy, and I can't afford a gift fit for a king.

MARY
That's all right. Come —

BOY
There's only one thing I can give, but it's the greatest gift of all.

MARY
… Love?

BOY
Music.

The BOY whips out a drum.

MARY
(alarmed)
Is that a drum?

BOY
(proudly)
You bet it is.

JOSEPH
(urgently)
No, no don't, please —

The BOY starts violently banging on his drum. Like, really pounding away. The baby starts wailing. MARY picks him up and rocks him, trying to quiet him.

DRUMMER BOY

MARY

Stop!

JOSEPH

You woke him up!

BOY
(stopping, delighted)

I think he likes it!

MARY

He doesn't like it. He's crying.

BOY

No, he smiled at me!

JOSEPH

He didn't.

BOY

I think he did.

JOSEPH

He definitely didn't.

MARY

What kind of sociopath plays a drum for a newborn?

BOY
(confused)

Are you mad at me?

MARY

Of course we are! We haven't slept since the day before Christmas Eve —

BOY

What is "Christmas Eve"?

MARY
— and we were finally about to get some sleep at last because the baby finally stopped wailing and the shepherds finally went away —

BOY
(disappointed)

I missed shepherds?!

MARY
But then you show up with a goddamn drum —

JOSEPH
You don't bang on a drum in front of a sleeping baby! What's wrong with you?

MARY
— and you ruined everything!

JOSEPH
(pointing at the drum)

Who bought you this?! Who bought you this drum?! I'll murder them!

Animal sounds start.

Oh great, you woke up the animals, too.

BOY
I think maybe you woke up the animals with your shouting.

MARY
Now Jesus will never get back to sleep!

JOSEPH
You IDIOT!

BOY
I'm the idiot?! You're the ones who had a baby in a barn!

MARY
There was no room at the inn!

BOY
Was there room at the hospital?

JOSEPH
Listen, you little jerk: You'd better get out of here before I throw you out.

BOY
You can't make me leave. You don't own this barn.

JOSEPH
Yes, I do.

BOY
(pointing)
You've got luggage in that corner with address tags saying you live in Nazareth. Why would you own a barn in Bethlehem if you live in Nazareth?

JOSEPH
I'm a real estate mogul.

BOY
You're a loser.

The BOY starts drumming again. The baby and animals wail louder.

JOSEPH
Stop banging the drum!

MARY
Where are your parents?

BOY
Where are _your_ parents? You're like fourteen.

JOSEPH
She's <u>fifteen</u>, and that's a perfectly reasonable age at which to have a baby!

MARY
Plus, this isn't just any baby; this is <u>God's</u> baby!

BOY
How does God feel about you having his baby in a barn?

MARY
There was no room at the inn!!

BOY
Also, you've got him sleeping in a trough. Animals put their dirty mouths in that thing, and that's where you decided to put God's baby?

MARY
He's fine.

JOSEPH
At least he was until you started drumming.

BOY
He could catch some disease and die.

MARY
He's fine. Go away.

BOY
I bet you'd feel pretty stupid if you killed God's baby.

MARY
We're not going to kill God's baby.

JOSEPH
That's right. We're going to raise him to adulthood, and then the Romans are going to kill God's baby.

                    BOY

Wait, what?

                    MARY

Just go away.

                    BOY

But I have a number of follow-up questions to that.

                    MARY

Look, kid. I haven't slept in two days, my boobs are leaking, and my genitals are torn to shreds.

                BOY & JOSEPH

Gross.

                    MARY

Go away before I kill you with your own drum.

                    BOY

Fine. I don't want to give your stupid baby a present anyhow. He's probably gonna grow up to be a jerk like you two.

> *He gives one last "pa rum pum pum pum" on the drum. Jesus and the animals start up again. His work done, the BOY turns to go.*

                    JOSEPH

Oh, come on! Did you have to —

> *The BOY whips back around to face JOSEPH.*

                    BOY

Yes, I did. I did have to.

> *The BOY exits as MARY tries to calm Jesus and JOSEPH tries to calm the animals.*

MARY
Shhhh, it's okay, Jesus.

JOSEPH
Shhhh, it's okay, animals.

The baby and the animals settle.

JOSEPH
Okay. Let's try for that nap again.

The BOY reenters.

BOY
Hey.

JOSEPH
Goddammit.

BOY
Just FYI, there's three guys outside who say they've been following a star for, like, ever, to meet your stupid barn baby, and if you're upset about the gift I brought, I really don't think you're gonna like theirs.

MARY
Are their gifts loud?

BOY
No.

MARY
Then we'll be fine.

BOY

If you say so.

The BOY starts to go, but then turns back.

You know, I'm gonna write a song about this.

JOSEPH

You're gonna compose a song on a drum?

BOY

You can compose a song on any instrument, you ignorant Nazarene. And I'm gonna paint you in a much better light than you deserve.

MARY

You're a rude little boy. Get out of here.

The BOY locks eyes with MARY and backs out of the barn, drumming the whole time. The baby and the animals begin wailing.

JOSEPH

That's it.

JOSEPH rushes toward the BOY, who turns and scampers off stage. JOSEPH chases him off.

JOSEPH

Give me the drum! Come back here and give it to me!

MARY tries to quiet the baby and the animals. JOSEPH reenters.

JOSEPH

He's faster than I thought he'd be carrying an instrument.

MARY

At least he's gone.

JOSEPH
So, since everyone's awake, do you want to just see these three guys right now?

MARY
I guess so. The sooner they come in and look at the baby, the sooner they'll leave.

JOSEPH
Maybe we'll be able to sleep in a couple of hours.

MARY
I hope so.

JOSEPH
I'll bring them in.

JOSEPH exits.

MARY
(to herself)
The angel didn't say it would be like this.

Blackout.

END OF PLAY

IMPERFECTLY FRANK

SETH FREEMAN

Reprinted by permission of the author.

For performance rights, contact Seth Freeman, seth.o.freeman@gmail.com

Synopsis
In trying to adapt the tradition of arranged marriage to today's possibilities, a family's best-laid plans spin wildly out of control.

Time
Now

Characters
INDIRA SINDHU, female, late 40s-60s, a mother

RAJEEV SINDHU, male, late 40s-60s, a father

FRANK SINDHU, male, 20s-30s, a son

JULIA JASWANI, female, 20s-30s, a girl

Setting
A tasteful living room

Estimated run time
10-12 minutes

IMPERFECTLY FRANK

Sindhu apartment in San Francisco. A view of the Golden Gate Bridge, if possible. Afternoon.

INDIRA SINDHU, dressed in a fine sari, is arranging a spread of food.

Her husband, RAJEEV, is setting out drinks.

Their son, FRANK, enters wearing crisp slacks, a clean shirt, sports coat.

INDIRA
Look at you. You look so handsome. Rajeev, doesn't he look handsome?

RAJEEV
Very nice indeed.

INDIRA
Your hair could use a little...

She wets her fingers, dabs at his hair, restyling it a bit.

FRANK
(pulling away)

It's fine, Mom.

INDIRA
I'm sorry if I'm excited. The Jaswanis are one of the finest Punjabi families in San Francisco. It's such an honor, such a compliment to you, Franklin, that they would accept our offer.

RAJEEV
I can hardly believe it, really.

INDIRA
It is all so perfect. You are smart, good-looking, interested in computers, in hiking, in movies. Michael Jaswani also likes computers, hikes in the mountains, the movies. A handsome boy. Very bright. You have so much in common.

FRANK

I'm sure he's very nice. But, Mom, first of all, this is America, and I don't want an arranged marriage.

INDIRA

An arranged marriage is not about what you want. That is the whole point. It is about what is best. The Jaswanis are exceedingly wealthy.

FRANK

Second of all, even if I were gay —

INDIRA

Ah, finally, you are admitting you could be gay —

FRANK

No, no. Not admitting. Not... gay. And, in case you haven't noticed, I'm not into money.

INDIRA

Even more reason to marry someone who has money.

RAJEEV

All we ask is that you respect this great tradition of our people, my son. It has worked very well for many centuries.

FRANK

Somehow, I don't think gay marriages were part of that tradition.

INDIRA

Of course not. They couldn't be.

FRANK

Okay, then —

INDIRA

Because until now, gay marriage was not possible.

IMPERFECTLY FRANK

RAJEEV
Yes. The new law is a game-changer.

INDIRA
Precisely. Now we are so much less limited in searching for the absolute best possible family with which to combine.

RAJEEV
There are twice as many possibilities. Double.

INDIRA
Which is why we were able to find this very fine family, Franklin.

FRANK
I respect our traditions, and I love you both, but you are still missing a rather basic element here: I am not now and have never been gay.

INDIRA
Tsk, darling. You will learn.

FRANK
Excuse me?

INDIRA
This is the way with our tradition. Often, the children resist at first. They think this is impossible; this cannot be. I am in love with some poor person, not the betrothed of the arrangement. They pine for this other person, believing, wrongly of course, that they could have been happy in their love and their poverty. For a little while. Then, when it is time to buy a house and buy a car and have all the things they want to have and to do all the things they want to do, they appreciate the wisdom of their parents.

FRANK
Perhaps in the old days, it worked out.

RAJEEV
Not perhaps, Franklin. It did work out.

FRANK
When the arranged marriages were all heterosexual.

INDIRA
Franklin, you are a bright boy. Don't you think that, over all the decades and centuries, there were people who were gay who were put in arranged marriages with people who were not gay?

FRANK
I guess so, sure.

INDIRA
If they could make it work, the opposite can work.

FRANK
Maybe those people were miserable.

INDIRA
They were happy.

FRANK
You can't know that —

RAJEEV
You will find, my son, that no marriage is perfect. Even your mother and I have not always gotten along perfectly.

FRANK
I don't think that wanting a spouse with the same sexual orientation is asking for perfection.

RAJEEV
Sex is just one part of the complex, wonderful, difficult, beautiful thing that is marriage —

FRANK
But it is not a little thing.

INDIRA
It is not little, but it is not so big, either, as American culture would make you think. All the fireworks and moving earth. It was never this thing of fireworks for me —

RAJEEV
Never, Indiraji?

FRANK
Please, you guys. Way, way too much information.

INDIRA
Better not to have unrealistic expectations.

FRANK
This is making no sense. Isn't Indian culture supposed to be conservative about sex?

INDIRA
A country with a billion people can't be that conservative about sex. At least, not all the time.

RAJEEV
The Kama Sutra — that was ours.

INDIRA
And we worship a goddess with eight arms. Who knows where she puts all those things?

FRANK
But don't you want grandchildren?

INDIRA
You and Michael can adopt.

RAJEEV
There are many nice gay families with adopted children in San Francisco.

FRANK
Don't you want grandchildren with your DNA, if it's possible?

INDIRA

You can do surrogate.

RAJEEV

We can find a nice Indian girl. Your seed —

FRANK

Please. Guys. I can't have my parents talking about my "seed."

INDIRA

Okay, but you get the point.

FRANK

No, I don't. I don't get it, and you obviously don't get it.

Getting a bit strident

I've been trying to be polite and respectful, but you have to understand: this is crazy and impossible.

INDIRA

Franklin, please! Now is not the time. The Jaswanis are on their way.

FRANK

It doesn't matter where they are.

INDIRA

They will be here any moment.

FRANK

This is not going to happen!

INDIRA reacts as if shot, pressing her heart with her hands.

INDIRA

Oh.

Staggering back

You wound me, Franklin.

FRANK

I wound you?

INDIRA

You are killing me, Franklin.

She slumps to the couch in a dramatic swoon.

Such grief, I cannot survive. Such shame, such disappointment. I will stop eating.

FRANK

Mother, you'll eat.

INDIRA

Never. Never again. Not a crumb will pass these lips. I will die.

FRANK

You're threatening a hunger strike if I don't have a gay marriage?

INDIRA

If you don't make a good marriage, this marriage which is all arranged. We cannot, at this point, insult the Jaswanis. Truly, it would be more than I can bear.

RAJEEV

It would be a terrible, terrible embarrassment, Franklin.

FRANK

Embarrassment? And what would you call what would happen on the wedding night?

INDIRA
Please, darling, that is private, between you and Michael.

Frank clasps his head.

FRANK
Ay! I am not hearing this.

RAJEEV
We are on a course now, Franklin.

FRANK
And you expect some Bollywood ending? Two hundred people in colorful clothes happily dancing in the streets?

RAJEEV
(picturing it)
That would be nice.

FRANK
Ay!

SFX The doorbell rings

INDIRA
Oh.

She pulls herself up, stands, and starts smoothing her sari.

RAJEEV
Okay, Franklin. Polite behavior, please.

INDIRA
(wiping her eyes)
Don't embarrass your family.

RAJEEV opens the door.

RAJEEV
(somewhat surprised)

Hello.

JULIA

Hello. May I come in?

RAJEEV

Of course.

JULIA, a pretty girl of Punjabi extraction, about Frank's age, enters.

JULIA

I am Julia Jaswani, Michael's sister.

RAJEEV

We are pleased to meet you. This is my wife, Indira, and my son, Franklin.

INDIRA

How do you do?

FRANK nods

JULIA

I won't stay long. We've had a rather stressful morning at our house, and my parents were too distraught to come themselves, so they sent me.

INDIRA

I am so sorry. What has happened?

JULIA

I'm afraid I have to convey a rather embarrassing bit of information from my family. Michael came out to us this morning. As straight.

RAJEEV

He is not gay, but you thought he was gay?

JULIA
He has always been very sensitive. He likes opera. He dresses well. And, well, you know, today it is perfectly all right to be gay.

INDIRA
Perfectly.

RAJEEV
Of course.

INDIRA
But is it not all right also not to be gay?

JULIA
Sure. But he thinks that, therefore, he should not be in a gay marriage. I'm afraid he is adamant. He refuses to go forward with this.

FRANK
I'm liking this guy.

INDIRA
See, son, I told you. You have so much in common.

FRANK
Ay.

JULIA
I feel terrible having to tell you this.

FRANK
I, at least, am very glad that you did.

JULIA
I'm so sorry. I was very much looking forward to meeting you, Franklin. I've heard such great things about you.

FRANK
False advertising.

JULIA
I think not. We have a lot of the same interests, I understand. Anyway, I'm sorry about all this, but... don't shoot the messenger.

FRANK
No, no. It's a good message.

JULIA
It is?

INDIRA
Franklin!

FRANK
There's no shame today in saying it. Julia, actually, I am also not gay.

JULIA
Oh.

FRANK
And I had told my parents that this... arrangement couldn't go forward.

JULIA
Oh. Well. Wow.

FRANK
Yes. So your parents should not feel so bad.

JULIA
They shouldn't, but... good luck with that.

FRANK
Tell me about it.

JULIA
Well, I'm sorry it had to be under these circumstances, but it was nice to meet you all.

RAJEEV

Nice to meet you.

INDIRA

Yes, quite nice. (*beckoning RAJEEV*) Rajeev. Please.

> *As FRANK and JULIA watch, puzzled, INDIRA steps downstage. RAJEEV follows. They put their heads close together, speak in low tones.*

Why did we not know about this sister?

RAJEEV

Maybe she is already promised.

INDIRA

And maybe she is not. She is quite pretty, I think.

RAJEEV

And intelligent, yes?

INDIRA
(smiles)

You see, Rajeev. We have a good marriage because we know without saying what the other one is thinking.

(more loudly, yet gently) Julia?

JULIA

Yes.

INDIRA

We have so much food here. Would the messenger like to stay for lunch?

JULIA

If that would be all right, yes, I would. Franklin, would you mind if I stayed?

FRANK

Please, "Frank." Only my parents call me Franklin.

JULIA

Frank.

FRANK

Yes, Julia. I would like that very much.

He turns to face the audience.

So, maybe this story will still have the ending we know you have been hoping for in your hearts...

SFX lovely, rhythmic Indian music.

INDIRA, RAJEEV, FRANK, and JULIA line up shoulder to shoulder. Suddenly, they each have little metal cymbals on their fingers. They dance to the lively music in the stylized, choreographed manner of the finales of Indian musicals.

Blackout

END OF PLAY

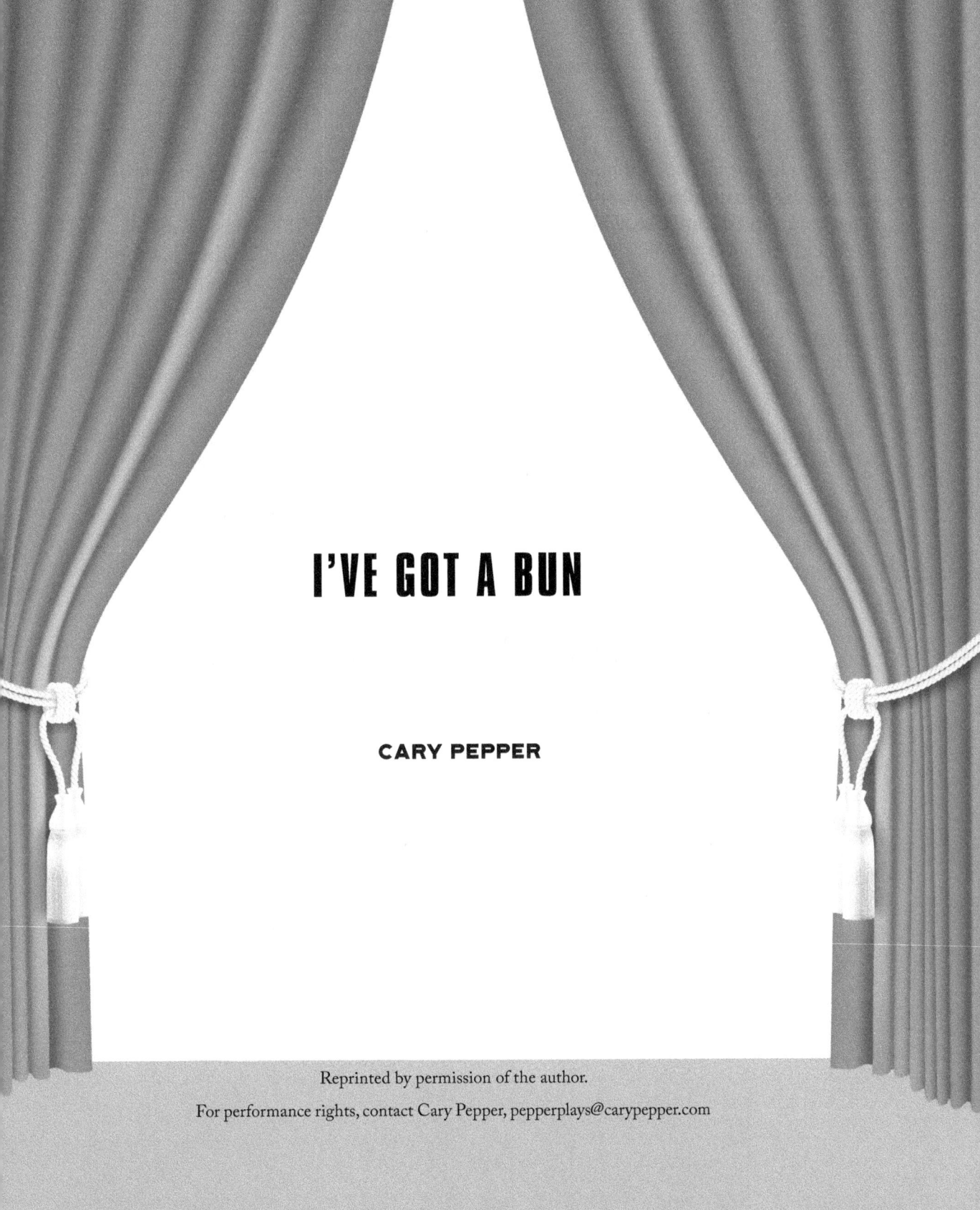

I'VE GOT A BUN

CARY PEPPER

Reprinted by permission of the author.
For performance rights, contact Cary Pepper, pepperplays@carypepper.com

Synopsis
Mason has been cast in a newly discovered, never-before-seen play by the world-class absurdist, LaSalle Montclare. But the play must be performed exactly as written. And Montclare, who worked on a typewriter when there was no spell check, was a lousy typist. This is why the play opens with Mason holding his co-star at gunpoint and having to say, "I've got a bun. Come out or I'll hoot."

Time
The Present

Characters
JOHN: Male. A theatre director. Age is unimportant, but probably at least 40.

MASON: Male. An actor. Age is unimportant, but should be about the same age as John.

Setting
A rehearsal space. Could be a big empty space, could be John's apartment.

Estimated run time
10 minutes

I'VE GOT A BUN

[Note: Line breaks are intentional and reflect the rhythm of the dialogue.]

A rehearsal space. JOHN is already there. MASON enters.

JOHN
Mason! Good to see you again. Thanks for signing on.

MASON
Thanks for asking me.

JOHN
I wanted you for this part from the moment we got permission to do the play.
Didn't even ask anyone else.

MASON
Didn't even ask me to audition!

JOHN
Didn't have to. Far as I'm concerned, this is your part. Gloria Fulton's agreed to do the other role.

MASON
Great! I always like working with her.
Gloria puts her all into everything she does. Never holds back.
Once, I was supposed to slap her, and she insisted I actually do it.
She wouldn't let me fake it. She is so committed.

JOHN
She said the same about you. So we're already in great shape.
She'll be late today, but you and I can do a read-through. I'll read in for her.

MASON
Okay.

JOHN
You know how lucky we are to get this? A play by LaSalle Montclare that the world has never seen!

MASON
I thought all his plays have been done.

JOHN
So did everyone else. It's one of those long-forgotten works, discovered-in-the-attic kind of things. I don't think we'll have to worry about full houses!
Ready to start?

MASON
Sure. But I haven't read the script yet.

JOHN hands him a script.

JOHN
Sorry about that. The estate is putting all sorts of restrictions on the production. They're being very fussy about the script not being seen before the show opens, so they're monitoring all copies of the play.

We'll just do a cold read and take it as we go.
The play opens where you're threatening Gloria's character.

MASON
(reading)

I've got a gun!

JOHN
Uh, that's not what the script says.

MASON
I know. It says, "I've got a bun." But that's obviously a typo.

JOHN
I agree. But we have to perform the play exactly as written. Every word. It's in our contract with Montclare's estate.

MASON
But it's a typo.

JOHN
I told you, the estate is being... did I say fussy? Try dictatorial. On steroids. If we don't perform the play exactly as Montclare wrote it, they'll pull production rights. They made that very clear.

MASON
That can't apply to typos.

JOHN
That applies to everything.

MASON
Did you know this when you agreed to direct?

JOHN
Yes, but I didn't know it was written this way. Turns out, all his scripts are written like this. Montclare might have been a brilliant satirist, but he was a lousy typist. And he wrote all his plays on a typewriter. So, no spell check.

MASON
You're going to have me holding a bun onstage?

JOHN
That's what's in the script.

MASON
And Gloria's going to be scared of that?

JOHN
Yes.

MASON
Why?

JOHN
Because it's in the script.

MASON
Why would someone be scared of a bun?

JOHN
Let's deal with that when we talk about the characters' backstories.

MASON
I won't do it.

JOHN
You have to do it. It's in your contact with us.
Clause #15 — You agree to perform the script as written.

MASON
You're threatening me with a contract?

JOHN
If I don't, the producers will. They really want to do this play.
Let me ask you something. You've read Montclare's work. Didn't you know what you were signing on for?

MASON
Yes, but bizarre language was always in the dialogue. It never involved what characters <u>did</u> on stage. I've never seen anything like this in any of his plays.

JOHN
This is an early piece. Maybe he became a better typist.
From the top?

MASON
(reading)
I've got a... bun

JOHN
(reading)
Don't hurt me!

MASON
(reading)

Then come out of there, or I'll...

You can't be serious.

JOHN

Contracts... Stipulations...

John reads.

Don't hurt me.

MASON
(reading)

Come out, or I'll... hoot.

JOHN

How are you going to hoot?

MASON

What do you mean?

JOHN

When you hoot, what do you intend to do?

MASON hoots softly.

JOHN

That's not very intimidating.

MASON

Of course, it isn't. Obviously, it's supposed to be "I'll shoot." Hoot isn't intimidating!

JOHN

Not the way you're doing it.

MASON
Well, how would you do it?

JOHN
I don't give those instructions to my actors. That would be insulting.

MASON
You don't think <u>this</u> is insulting??

JOHN
Reach into your toolbox and find the right instrument.

MASON
Reach into my toolbox??

Can I at least screech or scream instead? At least I'd have something to work with.

JOHN
Sorry. You'll have to hoot.

MASON
How about if I shout?

JOHN
It says "hoot."

MASON
But it's supposed to say "shoot." Obviously, a typo. Shoot — hoot. It could have just as easily been shoot — shout.

JOHN
But it isn't.

MASON
So I have to hoot.

JOHN
That's what it says.

MASON hoots.

JOHN
Still not intimidating.

MASON
I'll work on it.

Can we move on?

JOHN
From the hoot.

MASON hoots.

JOHN
(reading)
You kissed me!

MASON
John!

JOHN
That's what it says.

MASON
How could I have kissed her? I'm nowhere near her. And why <u>would</u> I kiss her?

JOHN
You're a crazed killer. You do unexpected things.

Moving on.

MASON
(reading)
Then I'll hoot again.

He hoots.

JOHN
(reading)

You pissed!

When she says that, look at the audience, then look down at your pants.

MASON

Why?

JOHN

You're checking to see if she's right.

MASON

About what??

JOHN

That you just pissed. I interpret that to mean you've pissed yourself.

MASON

Why would I do that?

JOHN

You're nervous.

MASON

About what?

JOHN

I'll let you decide that.

MASON

How about if I decide it didn't happen?

JOHN

But she just said it did.

MASON

I don't think I can do this.

I'VE GOT A BUN

JOHN
It's a long-lost script by a brilliant writer that's never been done before.
It's going to be a sell-out. A huge hit. Are you sure you want to turn that down?

MASON
You don't think we're going to get laughed off the stage?

JOHN
I think we're going to get nominated for a Tony.

MASON
I think you've lost your mint!

JOHN
My mint?? What are you talking about?

MASON
It's a typo. I was saying you've lost your mind.
But substitute one letter, and that's what you get.
Like we're getting here. We both know what the playwright was really trying to say.

JOHN
And we know what the playwright wrote.

MASON
Only because he couldn't hype.

JOHN
What??

MASON
Type! He couldn't type!
Why don't we do it without the mistakes? At least it'll make sense. If we perform this, we'll get laughed out of the business.

JOHN
Do you know what they said about the last Montclare play that was done? The one about Jesus — "He Vied for Our Fins."

He takes out clippings and reads.

JOHN
"Montclare is a world-class absurdist with an amazing ear for language who turns society's foibles squarely on their heads with devastating comic effect."
That was "The New York Times."

In London, they said, "A hilarious play by a courageous artist for whom nothing is sacred, this masterpiece takes the audience on a wild ride during which everything people think they know is thrown back at them in what sounds like nonsense but soon strikes home as deftly-created social commentary."
Our production is going to be named in reviews like those.

MASON
But this is… You're saying the estate is insisting on this?
Why would they want <u>this</u> to be his newly-discovered masterpiece?

JOHN
The estate feels his literary reputation is based on his signature style. It's what established him as…

MASON
A playwright who couldn't type?

JOHN
A world-class absurdist for whom nothing is sacred. You know, he ran his goldfish for mayor of his town.

MASON
He was that crazy?

JOHN
He was that good. The goldfish won.

The estate doesn't want his reputation tarnished or sullied. Their words. So, moving on… It begins to escalate. You approach her.

MASON

We are not doing the next stage direction as written.

JOHN

We have to. It's in the contract.

MASON

Have you read it?

JOHN

Yes.

MASON

Well, I haven't. Until now. Otherwise, I never would've taken this part.

JOHN

But you did take the part.

MASON

But I hadn't read the script. And if I did, I'd've assumed this was a typo, which we would fix.

JOHN

But we can't.

MASON

Well, we certainly can't perform it as written. Especially with Gloria. She'll...

JOHN

We have to perform it as written.

MASON

You have to be kidding. This isn't one typo. It's several!
It's clearly supposed to mean "She knocks him into the wall."

JOHN
So, you approach her... And she kicks you in the balls.

MASON
JOHN... !!!

Blackout

END OF PLAY

SANTA NOIR

JAMES McLINDON

Reprinted by permission of the author.
For performance rights, contact James McLindon, jmclindon@gmail.com

Synopsis
Santa pauses on his rounds for a snack... and comes face-to-face with his darkest secret.

Time
The Present

Characters
SANTA, male, probably appears to be 50s-80s. An ancient elf with belly and beard.

NOELLE, female, 18, a rebellious young goth.

DONNA, female, mid-20s to mid-30s, sexy and enticing.

Setting
The living room of a modest apartment on Christmas Eve. A fireplace with a mantel is a nice touch.

Estimated run time
10 minutes

SANTA NOIR

Christmas Eve, late at night. A tired SANTA leans against the fireplace mantel, savoring a cigarette and a glass of scotch. NOELLE sits watching him, obscured by the shadows. A film noir sensibility should be evident throughout.

SANTA

You never forget my snack, do you, Donna? (*after a long drag*) Thanks. So… is this the year?

NOELLE

How's the scotch?

SANTA

Outstanding. Single malt.

NOELLE

Single malt, <u>neat</u>. And a Marlboro.

SANTA takes a savoring sip.

SANTA

Is this 10-year-old Laphroaig? Wait, is it the 18-year-old?

NOELLE

You deserve it.

SANTA

Yeah, well, Donna, we both know that isn't true.

NOELLE

You're the most generous man in the world. Every year, every child in the world gets exactly what they want. Every single child. (*pause*) Except one.

SANTA

Except one? I never miss anybody.

NOELLE

You always miss one. Every year. (*moving into light, revealing for the first time that she is a goth*) Don't you?

SANTA

Who are you? You sound just like Donna — (a *long pause*) Noelle.

NOELLE

Noelle. Hello, Santa.

SANTA

I guess this is the year. But where's Donna?

NOELLE

She passed away last month. Cirrhosis of the liver.

SANTA drops into a chair and sighs.

SANTA

Oh… wow. Did she suffer much?

NOELLE

No more than anyone in this world suffers. So, yeah, quite a bit. (*pause*) I know who you are.

SANTA

Everyone knows who I am.

NOELLE

That is, I know who Mom said you are. She told me the whole story right at the end. It sounded crazy and, well, Mom did lie some. So, I decided to stay up late tonight, put out the scotch, and see for myself.

SANTA

What story?

NOELLE

Is that really how you want to play this?

A long pause. SANTA hangs his head.

SANTA NOIR

SANTA
Damn.

Lights down over NOELLE. A time shift. A much less hardened SANTA, still an innocent elf, distributes presents under the tree. DONNA appears. She enters in a nightgown and watches him. A saxophone riff plays. Her voice is husky, sexy, breathy, as smooth as the scotch in her hand.

DONNA
Hello, Kris.

Startled, SANTA jumps, then turns to face her.

SANTA
Oh. Gosh. You're, you're not supposed to see me.

DONNA
(holding an unlit cigarette)
Ahhh. Dear Santa, it wasn't my fault. You make a surprising amount of noise for an elf, and I thought someone had broken in. Give a girl a light?

SANTA
I, I don't have any matches —

DONNA produces a lighter. SANTA hesitates, then takes and flicks it. She holds his hand as she lights her cigarette. It is very intimate.

DONNA
I've been waiting up for you.

SANTA
That's… that's kind of naughty.

DONNA
Yes, well, I'm kind of naughty. But you know that. Don't you?

SANTA
Look, no one is ever supposed to see me.

DONNA
It's all right, Kris. No one has to know.

SANTA
Know what?

An uncomfortable (for SANTA) pause.

DONNA
There's something you're hungry for? Isn't there?

SANTA
Um, well, I can always go for some milk and cookies.

DONNA
I was thinking scotch and Marlboros.

SANTA
What's scotch and Marlboros?

DONNA
They're like milk and cookies. For grown-ups.

SANTA
I don't really know what that means.

DONNA
Milk and cookies. That've had a hard life. A life full of excess and pain and thrill and experience.

SANTA
I don't know what that means either.

DONNA

The only way to really learn about something… is to taste it. Would you like to taste it?

SANTA

Ummm…

> *DONNA holds the glass to his lips. Against his better judgment, SANTA sips.*

SANTA

Oww. It burns.

DONNA

Just like life. It burns so good. It burns right through you. It burns away every bad thing you've ever done.

SANTA

I've, I've never done anything bad. I'm Santa Claus.

DONNA

If you drink enough of it, no matter what you've done, it will cleanse you and make you feel pure again. Would you like some more?

SANTA

No. (*off her look*) Yes. Please.

> *She holds the glass to his lips like a chalice. He sips.*

DONNA

My turn.

> *She seems about to kiss him. Perhaps SANTA braces for the kiss. Instead, she sips the scotch.*

DONNA

When you know the antidote to doing something bad, you're free.

SANTA
Free? To, to do what?

DONNA
Something bad. Would you like to do something bad with me?

SANTA
No! I don't! I told you, I'm Santa.

DONNA
Isn't lying bad? Because you just lied to me. So I'll ask my question one more time: Do you want to do something bad with me? Or is that just a big, old lump of coal in your... stocking?

SANTA
I... I... I...

DONNA stills him with a finger on his lips.

DONNA
Shhhhh, baby. Hush.

DONNA begins to kiss SANTA. (Both actors can move towards each other in their Zoom windows and turn their heads away from us. Perhaps surrogates in shadow are used as stand-ins.) At first, he resists, then returns her kisses passionately.

They sink to the floor. The jazz riff plays again. Lights down over them. Time shifts back. Lost in the past, SANTA swirls his scotch, then finishes the glass.

SANTA
She made a man of me right there under the Christmas tree. Well, technically an adult elf, but you get (the idea) —

NOELLE
Yeah, eww, I get it.

SANTA

I used to be a happy-go-lucky guy. Even for a pixie. But not since Donna. She made it all seem free, easy, no consequences. But everything has consequences. The kind that haunt an elf.

NOELLE

If you were so haunted, why didn't you ever ask to meet me?

SANTA

But I did. Donna wouldn't let me. Every year, she said you couldn't handle it yet. That she'd tell me when you were ready.

NOELLE

I could have handled it. Why did you let her make the rules?

SANTA

I guess she kinda set that pattern the first time we met. Look, I'm just a sprite. What do I know about women? Or kids?

NOELLE

Said the person most beloved by children in the whole world.

SANTA

Yeah, I know if they're naughty or nice. I know what they want. But that's it. I've never even talked to one. (*pause*) Noelle, you don't know how much I've wanted to meet you. But your Mom was raising you alone. Who was I to tell her she was wrong?

NOELLE

You were my father! Who I knew nothing about. Until she told me just before she died.

SANTA

I guess I'd be mad, too, if I were you —

NOELLE

Don't you dare pretend you have any idea how I feel.

SANTA
Then don't you pretend you have any idea how I feel.

A pause.

NOELLE
Fair enough. How do you feel?

SANTA
Like a part of my soul was stolen. By your mother. And then another part. By you.

A pause.

SANTA
Okay, maybe I should've defied her. Maybe I shouldn't have been so afraid of you.

NOELLE
You... you were afraid of me?

SANTA
You were the most perfect thing in the world when you were born. Three months old, your first Christmas Eve, the only time I ever saw you. Just perfect. And I knew, right then, I had to let your mom raise you. Because I had no idea how. What if I messed you up? What if I ruined you? Oh, yeah, Noelle, you terrified me.

NOELLE
You were a coward.

SANTA
Maybe. But I never stopped thinking about you. Every year, the first name that I checked on my list was yours. I kept close tabs on you, kid.

NOELLE
Like how?

SANTA
I saw you when you were sleeping, I knew when you were awake, that sort of thing.

SANTA NOIR

NOELLE

That's kind of creepy.

SANTA

It's horrifying. Some things you can't unsee.

NOELLE

Oh my god!

SANTA

No, no, not you. But jeez, kids these days. Like that Cory guy… I was so glad when you broke up with him last summer. That kid was trouble.

NOELLE

You knew about Cory? Even Mom didn't know about him.

SANTA

I know everything about you. You've always been nice, Noelle. It made me happy you were taking after me, not your moth — Sorry.

NOELLE

I know she wasn't very nice. She seduced Santa Claus, for god's sake. (*pause*) I thought you would be jollier.

SANTA

I was once. But some women, you never get 'em out of your system. I thought you would be… less into darkness and death. What's that all about? You used to be such a happy kid.

NOELLE

Well, what's your fascination with joy, generosity, and life all about?

SANTA

People need more of that.

NOELLE

People need death, too.

SANTA

Why?

NOELLE

Who wants to live forever in this world? Not every day is Christmas.

SANTA

It is where I come from. (*pause*) You know… you could join me.

NOELLE

Join you?

SANTA

You're half elf, you could. It would be nice to, y'know, get to know you.

NOELLE

What would I do there?

SANTA

Make toys. Sing carols. Bake cookies. That sort of thing.

NOELLE

Yeah, I don't really do that.

SANTA

Maybe you should start.

NOELLE

It hasn't done you any good.

SANTA

You have to work at joy, kid. That's one thing I've learned. After you grow up, it doesn't just come to you anymore. I stopped working at it a long time ago. Looks like maybe you have, too.

NOELLE

You shouldn't have to work at it.

SANTA
You could find it again. (*offering his hand*) We both could maybe. Together.

NOELLE
Don't.

SANTA
Why not? Try with me?

NOELLE doesn't respond.

SANTA
I've missed you, Noelle. Even without knowing you, I've missed you. So much.

A long pause.

NOELLE
How would I even get there?

SANTA
You just stand by the fireplace. And you put your finger on the side of your nose. Like this.

NOELLE
And what? I'd just fly up to your sleigh like you do?

SANTA
Yeah. You'd just fly up.

No response

It's the only thing I want for Christmas. It's the only thing I've wanted for the last 18 Christmases.

NOELLE
That's pretty unfair.

SANTA
Santa being unfair. That should tell you how much I want this.

NOELLE
I'll think about it. For next year, I mean.

SANTA
Yeah. Okay. Sure. (*pause*) Merry Christmas, honey. (*No response*) Okay, well —

NOELLE hugs him and kisses his cheek. Again, they move towards each other in their windows. Again, perhaps surrogates in shadow are used as stand-ins.

NOELLE
Merry Christmas. Dad.

NOELLE steps back awkwardly and then flees, exiting. A pause as a stunned SANTA watches her go, touching his face where she kissed him. SANTA smiles. The chortle that follows is loud and long and innocent and joyful.

SANTA
Next year. Ho, ho, ho, ho, ho! Ho, ho, ho, ho, ho! Ho, ho, ho — !

He puts his finger next to his nose. Blackout. A whooshing sound.

END OF PLAY

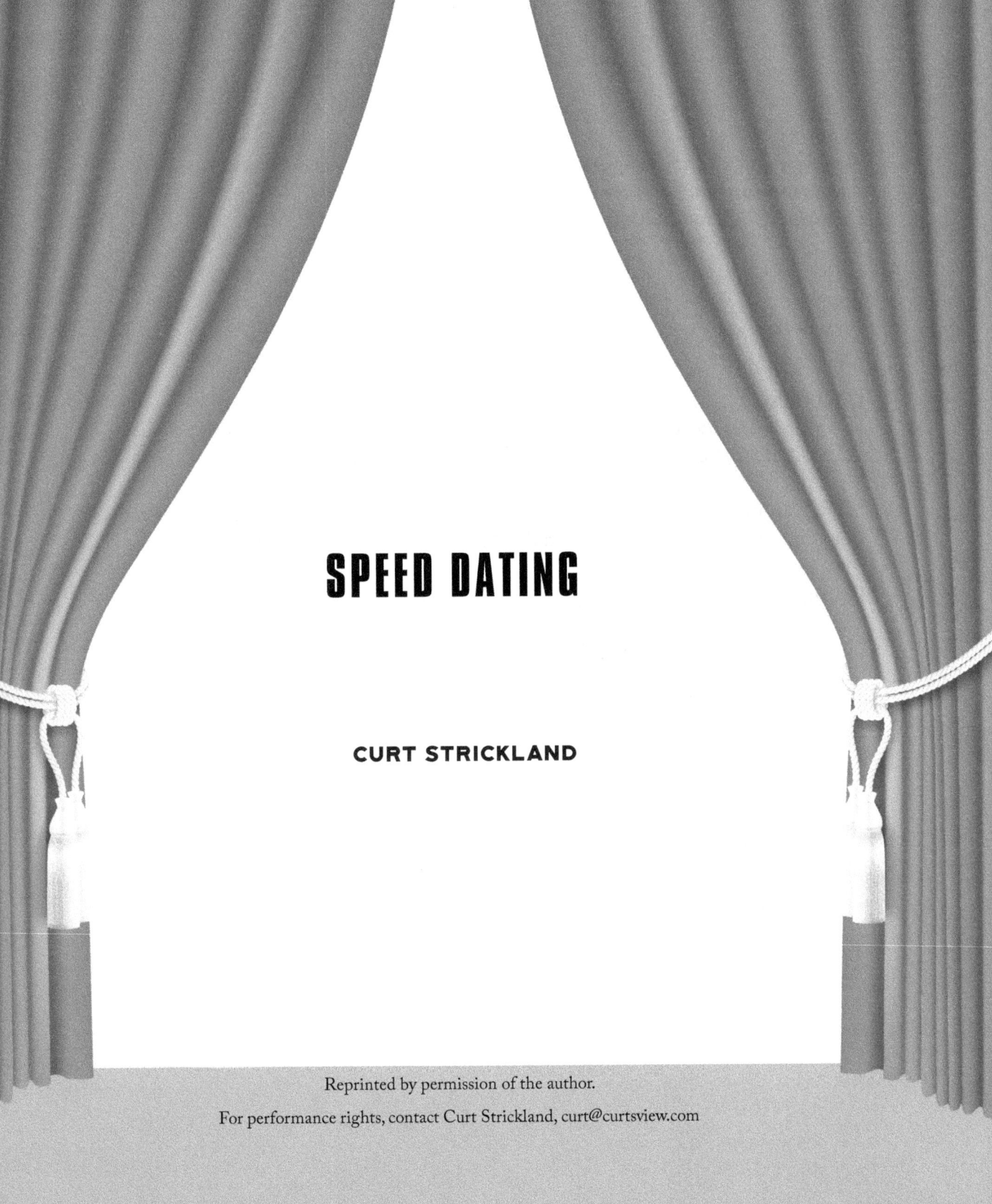

SPEED DATING

CURT STRICKLAND

Reprinted by permission of the author.
For performance rights, contact Curt Strickland, curt@curtsview.com

Synopsis
A widow and a widower — each deeply affected by loss — reluctantly attend a dating meetup in a hotel conference room, and their back-and-forth banter leads somewhere different than they expected.

Time
Present day

Characters
JESSE, around 65 years old, male, any ethnicity, tastefully dressed, with an easy-going manner and a kind smile. He is holding a water bottle.

SARA, around 60 years old, female, any ethnicity, attractive, her outfit is indicative of a sense of style. She is holding a drink.

Setting
The conference room of a Holiday Inn that is hosting a speed dating event for seniors. There is a fold-out table stacked with water bottles and brochures.

Estimated run time
12 minutes

SPEED DATING

They both have name tags. Jesse walks over to Sara, standing alone, nursing a drink.

JESSE

Hi, my name's Jesse.

SARA

I know.

JESSE

You know? Are you clairvoyant?

SARA

No, just able to read. I see your dog tag.

JESSE

Dog tag?

SARA

Yeah, your sticker.

JESSE

Oh.

A beat.

SARA

So, tell me about yourself. We got ten minutes, apparently.

JESSE

Well, I was recently widowed.

SARA

I'm sorry, how recent?

JESSE
(straight face)

Couple of days.

A beat.

SARA
So you're at the end of your grieving process. You seem to be holding up well.

JESSE
Hour thirteen was rough, but I got through it.

SARA
Is your wife actually in the ground, or did you blow off the burial?

JESSE
I'm not sure if they have tossed the dirt back in, not privy to the gravediggers' timetable, but for all intents and purposes, we can put a fork in that relationship.

SARA
Okay, to recap: officially single, wife's body may or may not be in the ground.

JESSE
I think ex-wife is the appropriate title.

SARA
Okay. Fair enough. So, tell me more about yourself. Are you still able to perform sexually?

JESSE
Whoa! Is that a first-date question?

SARA
Perhaps not. But at my age, I'm way beyond the court-and-spark stage.

JESSE
Fair enough. But you should know I recently had a double-lung transplant.

SARA
... Okay. I'm not sure I would have opened with that.

SPEED DATING

JESSE
Cards on the table. And if we end up getting married, you should know that my end-of-life scenario will not be romantic. I will slowly lose control of my faculties as well as my bowels. How do you feel about bowel clean-up on an aging husband?

A beat.

SARA
You haven't dated much, have you?

JESSE
First date in forty-five years.

SARA
No judgment here, but have you ever heard the concept "best foot forward"? Your end-of-life scenario, you might wanna keep that on the down-low, especially on a first date. But hey, that's just me.

JESSE
So, you're saying I have no game?

SARA
I've seen worse. You might wanna rethink the subjects you bring up for conversation.

JESSE
Like the bowel scenario?

SARA
Not a good visual. Now, just to confirm: your wife is dead, but not quite buried.

JESSE
Is that some kinda deal breaker for you?

SARA
Well, I do have standards. I generally insist that the men I date have their dead spouses in the ground, covered with dirt.

JESSE
She should be in the ground by now — just didn't want to be late for the speed date.

SARA
Okay. Let's review your pitch: you've been a widower for two days.

JESSE
Two and a half, actually.

SARA
Huge difference. At some point, you will lose control of your bowels which, if I was your wife, I would be expected to clean up.

JESSE
Well, no. At the first sign of a cold, you should immediately file divorce papers.

SARA
Okay, silver lining, exit strategy. I like that. So, in our marriage vows, we will replace " 'til death do us part" with "at the first sign of a cold."

JESSE
Bingo.

SARA
Anything else you wanna add?

JESSE
I'm not sure how set up I am financially. I might be relying on the kindness of strangers or my future wife.

A beat.

SARA
The hits keep on coming. Okay, let's review your pitch: a wife who has been dead for two days.

SPEED DATING

JESSE

Two and a half.

SARA

Changes everything. Okay. In the future, you may have lung complications, bowel issues, a shaky financial future, and a former wife whose body may or may not still be warm.

JESSE

What's not to love?

SARA

I guess you are a player.

JESSE

Thank you. So, tell me about yourself.

SARA

I lost my husband yesterday.

JESSE

Whoa! Nice you could fit this into your schedule.

SARA

Time management.

JESSE

On steroids. What else?

SARA

I may be a schizophrenic.

JESSE

Huge selling point with guys. It's like dating a different woman every night.

SARA

How exciting is that?

JESSE
Men love that. Keeps the relationship fresh.

SARA
Good to know. And, I'm ambivalent about sex.

JESSE
Guys love to hear that. Gives men a challenge — another huge selling point.

SARA
And I'm not sure if I like men now or women.

JESSE
Sexual ambivalence: Guys take that as a personal challenge.

A beat.

I shouldn't be telling you this, but men think that after one night with us, lesbians will march right back to the home team.

SARA
Well, I think the evangelicals would be very interested in this superpower. I doubt they are having much success with conversion therapy, and this sounds like a quick, effective, and economical solution to the lesbian outbreak.

JESSE
Absolutely. This could be my side hustle, and I'd be doing God's work. Evangelicals are gonna love me.

SARA
With God on your side.

JESSE
But I do have reservations about your big reveal: not sure if all that comes under the heading "best foot forward."

SPEED DATING

SARA
Wasn't sure.

JESSE
Well, you're shaping up to be quite the catch.

SARA
What can I say?

JESSE
Ambivalence about sex: can't emphasize enough what a winning hand that is with the guys.

SARA
Gives men a challenge.

JESSE
We love challenges. What else?

SARA
Well, I may have killed my husband.

A beat.

JESSE
Whoa! Cards on the table! But wait, doesn't that mean you will be doing jail time?

SARA
They can't prove a thing — covered my tracks really well.

JESSE
But if you didn't cover your tracks, the only sex I'll be having is through conjugal visits.

SARA
How romantic would that be? I'll even rustle up some prison candles for your visits.

JESSE
What a romantic you are.

SARA
Well, I might have to have sex with the prison guards to set that up.

JESSE
And that would increase the odds I get some kind of STD after my conjugal visits.

SARA
Living on the edge.

JESSE
Question: Will you be having sex with any other profession — just so I can give a heads-up to my doctor?

SARA
(*Indignant*) Oh my god. I'm not some kind of whore, if that's what you're implying. I do have standards; I would only have sex with prison personnel, no other profession.

JESSE
You reek of integrity.

SARA
Thank you.

JESSE
Let's review, make sure we check all the boxes. One: ambivalent about sex. Two: may be carrying an STD. Three: might be a lesbian. You may wanna keep that on the down-low. Four: may or may not have murder charges to deal with. That about cover it?

SARA
I think it's very clear; I won't be single very long.

JESSE
You'll be married before your husband's body turns cold.

SPEED DATING

SARA

Now, if we do get married, we'll have what is commonly referred to as an open marriage: I sleep with prison personnel, and you sleep with lesbians.

JESSE

All-American couple right there.

Long pause as they gather their breaths, staring at each other.

SARA
(serious)

Can I ask you a question?

JESSE

Sure.

SARA

When did your wife pass?

JESSE

Four years ago.

SARA

Tell me about her.

JESSE

... Well, she was the most giving, loving person you'd ever want to meet. The love she gave out on a daily basis to me, our kids, our grandkids, the people she worked with, our friends... I was blessed and humbled by her. I adored her, was in awe of her. She breathed love into any action she was doing. Her life was an art form. And she always saw the best in people and insisted I be the best I could be. She refused to let me settle. I'm a better man for it. I think of her every day, and how blessed I was to have spent forty-five years with this angel from heaven. God graced me with this woman. She made my life full.

SARA

She sounds wonderful.

JESSE
She was. How about yours? When did he pass?

SARA
Three years ago. He was my rock. No matter what was happening, he was always so calm and optimistic. He never let me go to the dark side. And he worshipped me... which I could never understand. He saw the goodness in me that I couldn't see. I was blessed with a daily dose of unconditional love. It filled and nourished my soul, made me feel I could do anything. How do you replace someone like that?

JESSE
... I guess you don't. How many years?

SARA
Thirty-five years. I got a hole in my heart bigger than the Grand Canyon.

JESSE
We were both blessed.

SARA
Heaven was kind to us.

A beat.

JESSE
... Hey, you wanna go for a drink?

SARA
And miss meeting all these men with pacemakers and oxygen pumps?

JESSE
If you can tear yourself away.

SARA
You buying?

JESSE

Well, if you may recall, until my lesbian side hustle kicks in, I'm on very shaky financial grounds.

SARA

I guess you're buying.

JESSE

I guess I am. OK, our first drink together. Have to snap a picture and put it in our scrapbook, maybe include one of your mug shots.

SARA

We got a scrapbook already?

JESSE

Absolutely. I know a good one when I see one.

He holds out his hand. She looks at it for a few beats and then takes it. They exit.

END OF PLAY

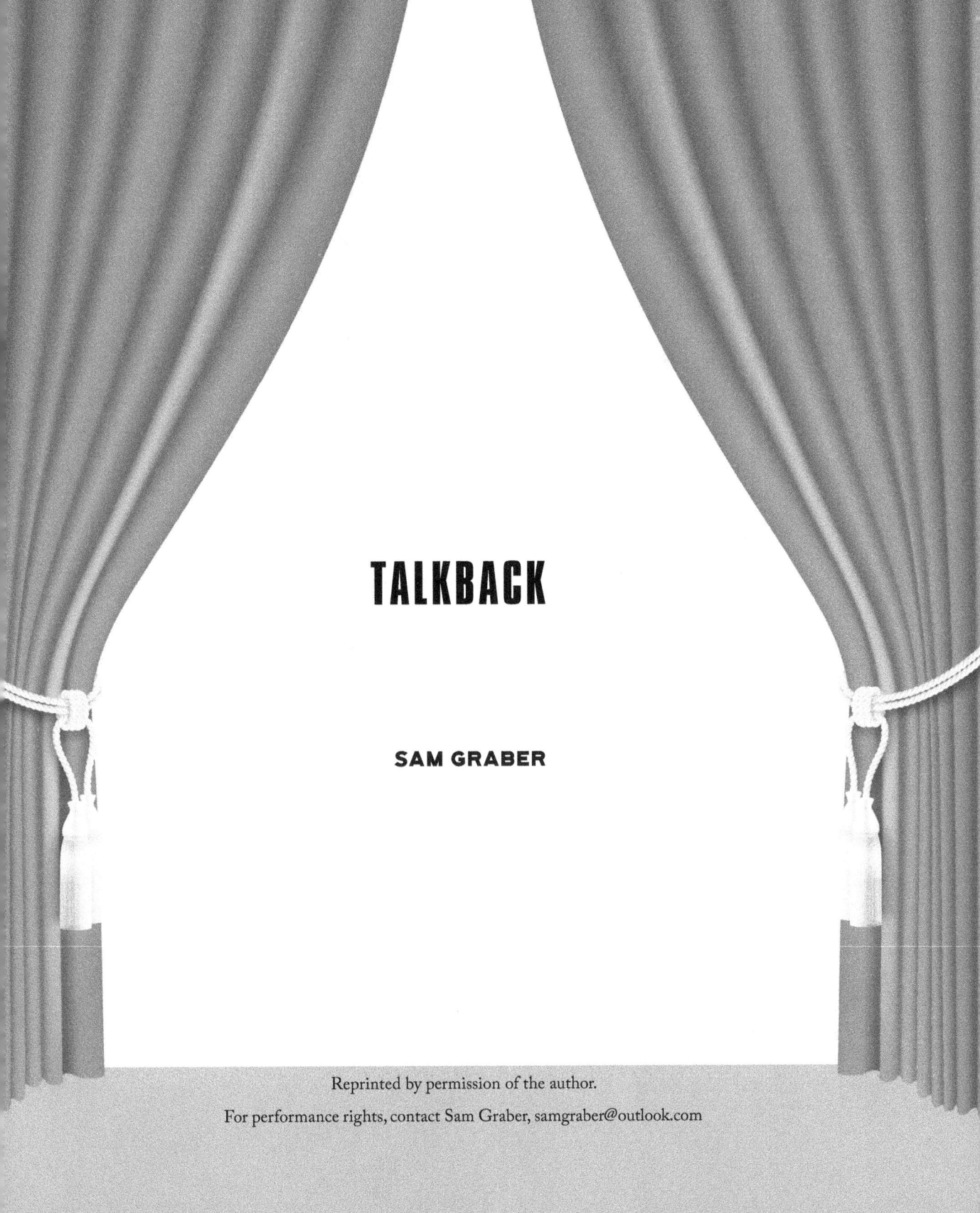

TALKBACK

SAM GRABER

Reprinted by permission of the author.

For performance rights, contact Sam Graber, samgraber@outlook.com

Synopsis
Having finished reading aloud the first draft of Hamlet, actors deliver feedback to the playwright.

Characters
JOHN, male, director

RICHARD, male, Hamlet

MARCUS, male, Ophelia

GEORGE, male, Laertes

THOMAS, male, Stage Directions

WILL is on stage but not embodied by a human actor. WILL is a cut-out, or puppet, or sad clown, inanimate.

Time / Place
1599, England

Estimated run time
7 minutes

TALKBACK

As lights come up, we see the cast in a sort of formation amongst themselves, reading off sheets of papers in their hands to JOHN and WILL, who are across and opposite them, watching the read.

THOMAS

A dead march. Exeunt. Bearing off the dead bodies. After which a peal of ordnance is shot off.
… curtain.
… the end.

There is a very long pause. At least five seconds of silence, after which actors might shuffle their scripts, clear their throats, squirm in their seats, look at the time.

They do not make eye contact with JOHN or WILL. It should appear to be highly uncomfortable for everyone.

Finally.

JOHN

Well. Um. Let's… take a break. Just to clear our heads. Collect-our-thoughts sort of thing. And then come back.

GEORGE

We've been here four hours already.

JOHN

I know, I appreciate it, <u>we</u> appreciate it, because it's new, and we needed to hear the words. All those words. From our esteemed playwright. We know it can be different to hear read aloud what we thought would be, you know, in our head. So let's quick break and then chat about… all those words.

Pause. Nobody moves.

GEORGE

I don't get it.

JOHN
Just take a quick break and then come back.

GEORGE
No. The play. I don't get it.

JOHN
Oh, um… maybe during the break we consider ways to ask our playwright questions in the form of… a question —

GEORGE
Like I don't mean to be rude and all. And I get it's a new draft. But I just don't get it.

JOHN
Right, well, that's why we're here, to have this read and talkback.

GEORGE
Like, I get what was happening and all, you know, the whole plot thing, but I guess…

JOHN
You don't get it.

GEORGE
Take the main character.

JOHN
Yeah.

GEORGE
His name's Hamlet.

JOHN
Yeah.

TALKBACK

GEORGE
And the dead father's name's also Hamlet.

JOHN
Yes.

GEORGE
They both have the same name.

JOHN
Yes.

GEORGE
I think you need a monologue to explain that.

Groans from the other actors.

GEORGE
Seriously, cuz otherwise, the audience thinks "Hamlet" is going to be about the dead King father Hamlet.

THOMAS
Has a point.

GEORGE
You have a play with two different characters sharing the same name, and everyone expects comedy. Took me until the play-within-a-play —

THOMAS
very not comedy —

GEORGE
—to go OHHhhhhh, it's about THIS Hamlet.

THOMAS (to WILL)
Did you not have a title?

JOHN

If we can just take a break —

RICHARD

May I say something?

JOHN

Christ, Richard, please. By the way, wonderful job.

RICHARD

Obviously. Except I'll need a very long break to restore my voice. My voice is my prized instrument, you know.

JOHN

Of course, Richard.

RICHARD

An instrument now frayed from overuse. I'm sorry, but how many words does the lead character need to say, "I'm a whiny brat and no one cares about me"?

Assents from the other actors.

RICHARD

It's not a sympathetic character. Privileged "upper crust" roams about the family castle yapping everyone's ear off about his problems? I don't want to bag on the words, mind you, it's poetic and all, but there's a damn lot of them.

Assents from the other actors.

THOMAS

Man needs to piss.

GEORGE

I'm pissing out my ears by the time these blokes are done smacking their lips.

RICHARD

Look, what you've tried to do here is...

TALKBACK

THOMAS
Ambitious.

RICHARD
And I'm sure you crushed plenty quill and blotter to scratch this all out, but you have too much speaking and not enough doing.

Assents from the other actors.

JOHN
Everyone, please, Will is a seasoned writer. He has the Queen's ear and the King's men. He knows how to take feedback. We're all on the same side here.

RICHARD
Fine: You need to show it instead of speak it.

Assents from the other actors.

GEORGE
The other stuff we've done: Shipwrecks! Teenage sex! This is all talking.

THOMAS
Out of order, too.

Assents from the other actors.

GEORGE
If it was me, I'd take Act V and make that your new Act I. Then we get the whole swordfight first, grabs the audience right away.

JOHN
But that wouldn't make sense.

GEORGE
Just make it all flashback, action up front, rest of it flashback.

RICHARD

But without all those words.

MARCUS

And my part. Ophelia.

JOHN

… yes?

MARCUS

Should be much bigger.

Groans from the other actors.

JOHN

Alright, everyone, let's take a break. I'll write down some leading questions to guide the conversation around areas which need attention.

MARCUS

Listen, Will, you know I don't like to talk about myself, but this Ophelia, I feel like my internal motivation is in conflict with what you've written here.

RICHARD

Just tell him what we're all thinking.

MARCUS

… I don't think you know how to write female characters.

Assents from the other actors.

MARCUS

Just because Richard here shows up in my room half-naked and crazed, I'm going to drown myself? I get the style is absurdist, but trying to seed the consciousness of women through drowning?

THOMAS

She should kill Hamlet.

TALKBACK

MARCUS
<u>There</u> we go.

RICHARD
Which Hamlet we talking about? Already-Dead-King-Father Hamlet or listen-to-me-whine-about-it-for-four-hours Hamlet?

MARCUS
What if I kill him in the new Act I?

Muttered interest from the other actors

JOHN
Look, let's respect that our friend and colleague here has been working on this piece for some time. Maybe we talk back to him on things in the play that really stood out to us. That made a positive impact.

GEORGE is scratching out lines in his script.

JOHN
George? What are you doing?

GEORGE
Crossing out stage directions.

JOHN
That's Will's first edition.

GEORGE
"After which a peal of ordnance is shot off." I don't need to know that, do I?

MARCUS
Not if <u>I'm</u> the one now pealing ordnance.

GEORGE
"Exeunt?" I mean: Do I <u>really</u> exit?

JOHN
No, you've just been stabbed with poison.

GEORGE
Oh, that's convenient. Look, fresh deaders, let's carry their bloody carcasses off... instead of burning them atop a pyre on!

RICHARD
Up the stakes, man!

GEORGE
Go like this: Curtain rises, bunch of half-naked madmen tossing dead bodies atop a pyre and lighting it up!

THOMAS
"Dead Hamlets."

GEORGE
There's your title.

RICHARD
And we stomp around while Marcus, as a sopping wet Ophelia, swordfights me as one of the dead Hamlets.

THOMAS
Queen don't like ghosts, tho.

RICHARD
But they're Danish ghosts, they don't count.

GEORGE
My religion prevents me being in a play with ghosts.

MARCUS
Look, I hate talking about myself, but I've always thought of my inner being as this constant reenactment of the silent power struggle in a society where certain people aren't allowed to contribute in meaningful ways.

TALKBACK

JOHN

Okay?

MARCUS

I think Rosencrantz and Guildenstern are gay.

Surprise from the other actors

GEORGE

My religion <u>really</u> likes being in a play with gay.

RICHARD

The bottom line is: This needs a nontraditional venue.

THOMAS

Site-specific.

GEORGE

Maybe out by those ring of stones in Wiltshire.

MARCUS

Maybe devised, Ophelia prompting words to guide the whole fire and swordfight thing.

GEORGE

But these words: Friending?… palmy?

RICHARD

You can't just make up words and expect <u>the instrument</u> to make them sing.

MARCUS

"Ophelia and the Dead Hamlets."

GEORGE

I mean, is this even really a play?

JOHN
ENOUGH!... now look!... you've all been very kind to provide your time and talent to reading this. And I get this is raw reaction, but really! Let's focus on being <u>con</u>-structive and not <u>de</u>-structive. Alright? I mean, it's not like we're sitting here criticizing <u>you</u>.

Long pause.

Then the actors stand and begin to hand in their scripts. After they hand in their sides, they each go off.

GEORGE
Just trying to help.

RICHARD
It's not that bad.

MARCUS
We'll do a workshop.

THOMAS
Ten-minute break then?

THOMAS exits, leaving JOHN and WILL.

JOHN (to WILL)
That went rather well, don't you think?

Blackout.

END OF PLAY

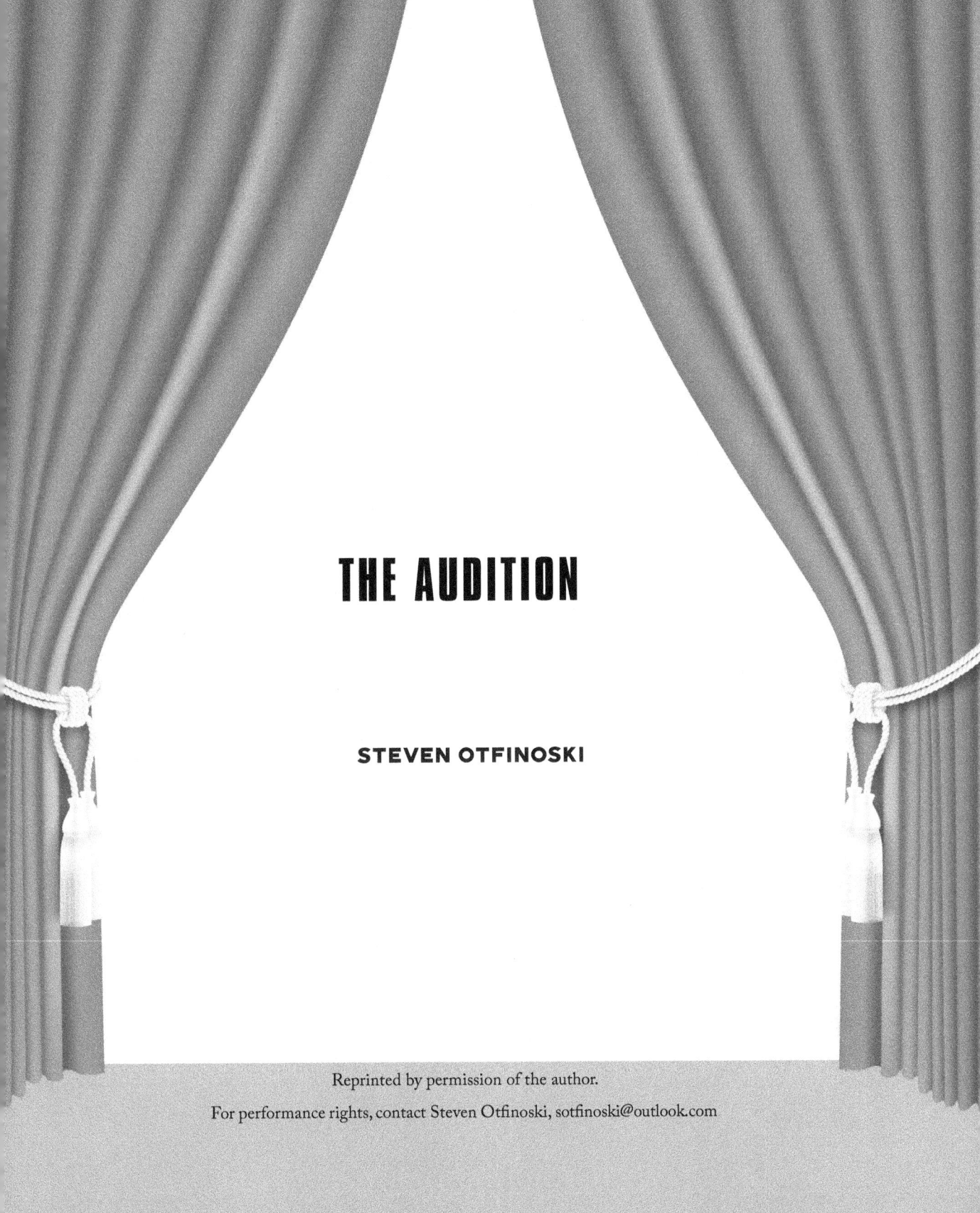

THE AUDITION

STEVEN OTFINOSKI

Reprinted by permission of the author.
For performance rights, contact Steven Otfinoski, sotfinoski@outlook.com

Synopsis
The director believed he had seen it all until Andrew Crawley came to audition. Surely his specialty of Off-Stage Acting is an act. Or is it?

Time
The Present

Characters
THE DIRECTOR, any gender, 30s-40s

THE ACTOR, male, 40s-50s

SECOND ACTOR, any gender, 30s-40s

Setting
A rehearsal room where actors are auditioning for a play. There are two chairs.

Estimated run time
10 minutes

THE AUDITION

DIRECTOR sits center stage holding a stack of resumes.

DIRECTOR

Next, please.

ACTOR enters, slightly overweight, nondescript.

Take a seat, Mr… Crawley.

ACTOR sits in chair across from DIRECTOR.

ACTOR

Thank you.

DIRECTOR
(referring to resume)

I see from your resume that you did "Waiting for Godot" last year at the Milwaukee Rep. What part?

ACTOR

I, uh, was Godot.

DIRECTOR

What?

ACTOR

I played Godot.

DIRECTOR

But, uh, Godot never appears. In the play.

ACTOR

No. He doesn't.

DIRECTOR

Then… how did you play him?

ACTOR
It wasn't easy. But then it never is.

DIRECTOR
(after a long beat)

This is a joke, right?

ACTOR
No. Of course not.

DIRECTOR
I'm afraid I don't —

ACTOR
Godot doesn't appear <u>on stage</u>. But his presence is felt throughout the play.

DIRECTOR
Well, that may be true. But there's no character. No lines. How can you play a character that the playwright hasn't written into the play?

ACTOR
Funny you should ask that. I've done "Godot" several times, and the first time I played it — I think it was at the Irish Rep — Samuel Beckett was in the audience. He came backstage after the show and told me — I'll never forget this — that I was the best Godot he'd ever seen. Well, of course, he'd never actually <u>seen</u> him, but it was his — my — presence that he was talking about.

DIRECTOR
Your presence?

ACTOR
You see, while it's true I wasn't actually <u>on</u> stage, I was there the whole time, just <u>off</u> stage.

DIRECTOR
You're there, off stage. For the entire performance.

THE AUDITION

ACTOR
That's right. They had a special chair for me in the wings. I could look out and see everything on stage. Didn't miss a thing.

DIRECTOR
But to what point?

ACTOR
Well, I'm acting, of course. Every moment.

DIRECTOR
Acting?

ACTOR
Reacting. Emoting. Being Godot.

DIRECTOR
Really?

ACTOR
Yes, you obviously have no experience with off-stage acting. It's much harder than acting on stage. When an actor is on stage, he has a whole arsenal of weapons at his fingertips to get across the character. His voice, body, movement, facial expressions, and so on. It's very different when you're acting off stage. You don't have any of those tools the on-stage actor can draw on. All you have to get yourself across is in here (*points to his heart*) and up here (*points to his head*).

DIRECTOR
I see. And who is feeling your… presence?

ACTOR
Well, the on-stage actors, for one. They're looking for Godot, and there I am in spirit, right smack in front of them. And gradually, over time, the audience feels my presence as well.

DIRECTOR
Even though they can't see you.

ACTOR
Let me explain it this way to you. There are plenty of productions of "Godot" that have no one playing Godot.

DIRECTOR
Uh-huh.

ACTOR
And there's nothing wrong with those productions. But they don't have that extra something, that dramatic spark that comes when there is a Godot in the wings, so to speak. If you, or even a casual theatregoer, were to attend a performance without Godot and one <u>with</u> Godot, you would immediately be able to tell the difference.

DIRECTOR
Really?

ACTOR
Oh, without a doubt. The power aura emanating from the actor. It's positively electric.

DIRECTOR
Uh-huh. Tell me, Mr. Crawley, do you make a career of playing these… non-existent parts in plays?

ACTOR
That's a patronizing way to put it. But yes, I am a trained off-stage actor.

DIRECTOR
(glancing down at the resume)
So, when it says here that you've been in a production of Clifford Odets' "Waiting for Lefty," you played the part of…

ACTOR
Lefty, that's right. That was a really tough one. I had to convey all the magnetism of the union organizer without actually appearing on stage. And then on top of that, I get shot and killed during the play. Off stage, of course. That took a lot out of me. I left the theatre every night physically exhausted, drenched with sweat.

THE AUDITION

DIRECTOR

And "Who's Afraid of Virginia Woolf?" Who did you play in that?

ACTOR

Virginia Woolf, of course.

DIRECTOR

Really?

ACTOR

That one was a real stretch. I was not only playing a woman, but a woman who was a famous author. And mentally unbalanced to boot. Talk about a challenge for an actor.

DIRECTOR

Now wait a minute. Virginia Woolf is barely even <u>mentioned</u> in the play. How could you possibly play a character that has no real presence in the play at all?

ACTOR

Oh, but you're wrong. Virginia's shadow hovers over the four characters the entire play. It is she who keeps upping the tension between George and Martha.

DIRECTOR

I thought that was the child that they never had.

ACTOR

Oh, I've played the child too. Much easier than old Virginia.

DIRECTOR

I'm afraid I'm finding this really quite absurd.

ACTOR

That's exactly what Albee said when he came to my dressing room after our final performance in Santa Fe. He had tears in his eyes as he cried out, "You've captured all the absurdity of my play."

DIRECTOR

Oh, <u>come on</u> now! This joke has gone too far.

ACTOR
I should have expected your reaction. The prejudice against off-stage acting is as bad as it is for any other minority group in the theatre.

DIRECTOR
What? Look. Even if I believed all this cock and bull you're throwing, I don't know why you came to audition. There are no parts or characters in this play that don't appear on stage.

ACTOR
That's not true. What about the doctor who's married to the leading lady?

DIRECTOR
What? He's only mentioned once in the entire play.

ACTOR
Well, he's no Godot, that's for sure. But times are hard for us off-stage actors, and I'm willing to do bit parts when I can get them.

DIRECTOR
He's not a <u>bit</u> part! He's not even a <u>speck</u> of a part!

ACTOR
(with sudden earnestness)
Give me a chance and I'll show you what I can do with him. In my hands, he'll be more than a speck, I can tell you.

DIRECTOR
I'm afraid there's nothing in our budget for actors who don't appear on stage.

ACTOR
I'm not proud. I'll take whatever you can afford. I'll do it for free, just to show you what I can do. It's just like that old theatre adage: There are no small parts, only small actors.

DIRECTOR
This <u>isn't</u> a small part. It's no part at all!

THE AUDITION

ACTOR

Oh, you know it all, don't you? Mister high and mighty big-time Broadway director! (*points finger at DIRECTOR*) Don't think the Off-Stage Actors' Guild isn't going to hear about this.

DIRECTOR
(long beat)

Wait a minute. Do that again.

ACTOR

Do what?

DIRECTOR

That expression and the finger-pointing.

ACTOR
(striking a pose)

You mean, like this?

DIRECTOR

That's it. Look, there's a small part of a waiter in the second act, I think you'd be perfect for.

ACTOR

Does he appear on stage?

DIRECTOR

Of course, he appears on stage. He's a waiter, for Chrissakes!

ACTOR
(after a thoughtful moment)

Nope. Sorry. I only do off-stage characters.

DIRECTOR

It's a paid part!

ACTOR

No, I have my standards.

DIRECTOR
Standards?

ACTOR
I wouldn't expect you to understand. And anyway, if the Guild found out, they'd blackball me. Sorry.

ACTOR begins to exit, turns back, walks up to DIRECTOR and takes his resume from his hand, turns, and exits.

DIRECTOR
(shaking his head)
And I thought I'd seen it all. (*Calling out*) Next, please!

SECOND ACTOR enters.

Have a seat.

SECOND ACTOR
Thank you. By the way, that fellow who just left. That was Andrew Crawley, wasn't it?

DIRECTOR
Why do you ask?

SECOND ACTOR
I caught his Godot last season in Milwaukee. God, he was good!

DIRECTOR
(long stare at ACTOR 2)
Tell me something before we go any further. Are you an on-stage actor or an off-stage actor?

SECOND ACTOR
Oh, I'm strictly on-stage. I don't have the chops for off-stage. I mean, how many actors do?

DIRECTOR continues to stare at SECOND ACTOR.

END OF PLAY

THE HOLIEST OF SACRAMENTS

PATRICIA CONNELLY

Reprinted by permission of the author.
For performance rights, contact Patricia Connelly, patricia.connelly.atty@gmail.com

Synopsis
Seven-year-old Molly Marie Fitzgerald is determined to make her First Holy Communion so she can keep her white dress and white pocketbook, but first, she must make a good First Confession. In order to do so, however, she must have sins to confess. Molly thinks she has a good, solid sin, but Father Hearn tells her otherwise. It's the end of a long, frustrating day for Father Hearn, and he tries to slide Molly through as quickly as possible. But Molly's Catholic school training is ingrained, and they reach an impasse. That is, until Molly has an idea. Will it work and allow her to make her First Holy Communion?

Time
The 1960s, around 6:00 PM, the evening of the day before the parish children make their First Holy Communion.

Characters
FATHER HEARN, male, 40s-60s, a Roman Catholic priest

MOLLY MARIE FITZGERALD, female, 7 years old*, smart, determined

*Molly may be played by a teen or older actor who can portray a seven-year-old.

Setting
The confessional in a Roman Catholic church. Normally, the confessional would have three sections. In the center section would be a large chair where the priest sits. On either side of the priest would be a small closet-like section with a kneeler, where individuals kneel to give their confessions through a screened opening in the wall. The screen, which can be opened or closed by the priest, allows the priest and confessor to converse privately without the confessor being visible. For the play, however, the confessional may be represented by a chair with arms for Father Hearn and a kneeler on one side for Molly. There should be a shelf or table near Molly.

Estimated run time
10 minutes

THE HOLIEST OF SACRAMENTS

The confessional booth in a Catholic church. FATHER HEARN is seated in the center of the confessional, waiting. MOLLY is kneeling in one of the confessionals on the side of the priest, occasionally looking around. FATHER HEARN looks up and rings a bell. Each time, the ringing becomes more intense, until finally:

FATHER HEARN

You know that when I ring the bell, you're supposed to begin?

MOLLY

Uh-huh.

FATHER HEARN

I've rung the bell several times, Missy.

MOLLY

My name's not Missy. It's Molly Marie Fitzgerald.

FATHER HEARN

Well, Miss <u>Molly Marie Fitzgerald</u>, this is an important day for you and your classmates. You are about to make your First Confession, and you have First Holy Communion tomorrow. These are the holiest of sacraments. This is the moment you accept Jesus and become an adult in the eyes of the church. Step One is to confess your sins and ask Jesus for forgiveness. Haven't you been taught that when I ring the bell, you should begin?

MOLLY

Uh-huh.

FATHER HEARN

Are you ready?

MOLLY

I don't know.

FATHER HEARN

Why not?

Silence. MOLLY squirms.

FATHER HEARN

There's nothing to be afraid of. When you finish, you'll be filled with God's grace.

MOLLY

But we're supposed to have <u>sins</u>, and I only have one.

FATHER HEARN

Is that the problem? It's perfectly fine your first time to have only one.

MOLLY

But Sister Agnes said <u>sins</u>.

FATHER HEARN

Confession is <u>my</u> job. I'm the one who has to be sure you make a good first confession, and if I say one sin is okay, then it's okay. So, you may begin.

Silence.

FATHER HEARN

You're the last one, Miss Molly, and we're way over time. If we don't finish soon, we'll both be in a lot of trouble. You don't want that, do you?

MOLLY

You forgot to ring the bell.

FATHER HEARN rings the bell. She hesitates, then —

MOLLY
(speaking rapidly, like a train barreling down the tracks)
Bless me, Father, for I have sinned. This is my first confession, and these are my sins —

She stops

See? I told you I'm supposed to have <u>sins</u>, Sister Agnes said, and you said one —

THE HOLIEST OF SACRAMENTS

FATHER HEARN
(interrupting)

Yes, I said one is enough. Go ahead.

MOLLY

Bless me, Father —

FATHER HEARN
(stopping her)

Only the sin, child. It's getting late.

MOLLY

This is my <u>sin</u>: I did something in kindergarten one time, and for these and all the sins of my past life, I am sorry, and for my penance, I will say three Hail Marys, thank you, Father. May I go now?

FATHER HEARN

Hold it! What was that?

MOLLY

My confession.

FATHER HEARN

I mean the sin. What was it?

MOLLY

I said it.

FATHER HEARN

You need to do it again, dear, and say what it was, so Jesus will hear it.

MOLLY

Jesus already knows anyway. Sister said.

FATHER HEARN

You still have to confess, which means saying what it is so I know.

MOLLY
Promise to give me only three Hail Marys for my penance if I say it?

FATHER HEARN
Miss Molly, you can't bargain with me, and you certainly can't bargain with our Lord.

MOLLY
But I can't do a Rosary. I don't have it, and I can't count that high for so many prayers.

FATHER HEARN
Who said you would have to say the whole Rosary as your penance?

MOLLY
Sister Agnes said the higher you go in commandments, the bigger your penance.

FATHER HEARN
I'm sure whatever you've done won't be high on the list of commandments.

MOLLY
It is.

FATHER HEARN
Tell me your sin and we'll see. Otherwise, I'll have to tell Sister Agnes you're not ready.

MOLLY
No, don't!

FATHER HEARN
Then show me you're ready. You do want to make your communion, don't you?

MOLLY
Yeah. If I don't, my mother will take back my white dress, and I won't get to wear it!

FATHER HEARN
You know there's more to communion than a white dress, don't you?

MOLLY
Oh. And the pocketbook.

MOLLY holds the white purse up to the screen.

See? My mother had to pay three dollars for it, and she doesn't have that kind of money.

(speaking rapidly — she's heard this from someone else) She's got to put food on the table. She's not made of money, especially for a dress I'll only wear once and a pocketbook I don't need. If I don't make my communion, she'll want her money back. So please don't tell me to say the Rosary because I can't do that penance and then —

FATHER HEARN
(cutting her off)
All right! All right! If you stop talking, you won't have to say a Rosary.

MOLLY
You promise?

FATHER HEARN
Excuse me?

MOLLY
YOU HAVE TO PROMISE!

FATHER HEARN
(silencing her)
Young lady! Don't yell!

MOLLY
(whispering)
And cross your heart and —

FATHER HEARN
(cutting her off)
Kneel down! Right now! You have ten seconds to finish or no communion tomorrow!

MOLLY
If I don't finish, can I still keep the pocketbook anyway?

FATHER HEARN
Put it on the shelf next to you! Right now! And don't touch it!

MOLLY
But I want to hold it.

FATHER HEARN
You can hold it when you're finished. Until then, I don't want to hear another word about the pocketbook. Go on. Do as I said.

She does. She tries not to cry, but can't help it.

FATHER HEARN
There's nothing to cry about. Kneel down like a young lady.

She kneels. Wipes her face. Church bells are heard.

FATHER HEARN
The six o'clock bells. Do you hear how late it is? Now please, let's get going.

Silence.

FATHER HEARN
Miss Molly?

MOLLY
You forgot to ring the bell again. Sister said we can't start until —

FATHER HEARN

Christ almighty!

He rings the bell hard.

MOLLY

Uh oh! You took God's name in vain!

FATHER HEARN

I know. I'm sorry. It slipped. But if you don't buckle down and say your confession —

MOLLY
(interrupting)

It's against the Second Commandment: "Thou shalt not take the name of the Lord thy God in vain."

FATHER HEARN

Yes, and I said I was sorry.

MOLLY

But do *you* have to go to confession?

FATHER HEARN

Of course.

MOLLY

Do you have other sins?

FATHER HEARN

Miss Molly, if you want the pocketbook, you better tell me your sin. Now!

The lights dim.

FATHER HEARN

You see that? The lights are dimming. That means someone will lock all the doors soon.

MOLLY
You have the key.

FATHER HEARN
Why would I need a key? I was supposed to be finished a long time ago.

MOLLY
Will we have to stay here all night?

FATHER HEARN
God forbid.

MOLLY
What will happen then if they lock the doors?

FATHER HEARN
I will take the secret passageway that only priests use and go to the rectory for my dinner. *(To himself in a low voice)* God forgive me.

MOLLY
(panics)
Would I have to stay here by myself all night? My mother won't know where I am, and what if she calls the police?

FATHER HEARN
You need to hurry up so that doesn't happen. Are you ready?

FATHER HEARN rings the bell long and loud. Silence.

FATHER HEARN
Miss Molly?

MOLLY
Then you're supposed to say, "You may begin..."

FATHER HEARN
GO! Or I will take the pocketbook and keep it for good!

MOLLY
(like a speeding train)

Bless me, Father, for I have sinned. This is my first confession, and this is my sin: I <u>committed adultery</u> one time, and for these and all the sins of my past life, I am sorry, and for my penance, I'll have three Hail Marys. Now I can take the pocketbook?

FATHER HEARN

Finally! That wasn't so hard —

Stops himself

Wait! Did you say you <u>committed adultery</u>?

MOLLY

(standing) Uh-huh. That's a sin. It's the Sixth Commandment.

FATHER HEARN slumps back in his seat as she waits.

FATHER HEARN

I've got the council waiting for me... A nice dinner. And here I am stuck with a seven-year-old who committed adultery.

MOLLY waits another moment, then —

MOLLY

Can I have my pocketbook now, please?

FATHER HEARN

Do you know what adultery is?

MOLLY

Uh-huh. I told you. It's the Sixth Commandment. "Thou shalt not commit adultery."

FATHER HEARN

But do you know what it means?

MOLLY

It's a sin of impurity.

FATHER HEARN

What else do you know about it?

MOLLY

It's dirty.

FATHER HEARN

Never mind. I'm sure you didn't commit adultery. It's something only adults do.

MOLLY

But I did. It was when I was in kindergarten. We were saying prayers, and I was trying to hold it, but we were standing for a long time when Sister went to the door, and we had to wait, and James made me look at him with a really funny face like this *(makes a face)*, and I couldn't hold it anymore.

FATHER HEARN

You wet your pants?

MOLLY

Uh-huh. I committed adultery on the floor.

FATHER HEARN

Wetting your pants is not adultery.

MOLLY

It is too. My uniform was dirty. It smelled. That's impure.

FATHER HEARN

No, child, you only commit <u>adultery</u> when you are an <u>adult</u>. See how that works?

MOLLY

You said I'll be an adult in the eyes of the church tomorrow, so by tomorrow —

FATHER HEARN

I know what I'm talking about! I'm losing my patience, young lady. Think of another sin! Hurry up! I don't want to have to tell Sister Agnes you're not ready!

MOLLY

I don't know any. I tried really hard to think of one.

She bursts into tears.

FATHER HEARN

Don't cry again! Tell me a sin! Any sin. Make something up.

MOLLY

That would be a lie, and it's against the Eighth Commandment to lie.

FATHER HEARN

Exactly what you need. It would give you two sins. The made-up one and the lie.

MOLLY

I'm going to tell Sister —

MOLLY runs out of the confessional and off stage.

FATHER HEARN

Wait! Come back! Don't go! I'll help you. We'll figure it out.

Nothing.

(*calling out*) Your pocketbook is still here on the shelf. What shall I do with it?

MOLLY enters and stops. She tries to speak, but can't. Silence. After a couple moments, she gathers up all her courage, then —

MOLLY

CHRIST ALMIGHTY!

FATHER HEARN
Wha —?

(a moment, as he realizes what she's done) Ah. Nicely done, Miss Molly Marie Fitzgerald. A perfect fit for three Hail Marys.

MOLLY
Now, can I —?

FATHER HEARN
Not yet. May our Lord Jesus Christ absolve you; and by his authority, I absolve you of your sins in the name of the Father, and of the Son, and of the Holy Ghost. Amen.

MOLLY
Now, may I have it?

She reaches for it, and he stops her.

FATHER HEARN
Wait. One more thing. Remember, confession is a secret between you and me and God. That means you can't tell anyone anything I said, and I can't tell what you said. Ever.

Indicating where the pocketbook sits

Otherwise, I may have to speak with Sister Agnes...

MOLLY
I promise. Do you?

FATHER HEARN
Cross my heart and hope to die.

MOLLY takes the pocketbook off the shelf, and they exit together as the lights in the church go off.

END OF PLAY

THE HOLIEST OF SACRAMENTS

Production Notes:
Set pieces:
Large chair, possible Captain's chair for Father Hearn

Kneeler or small chair

Shelf or table next to the small chair or kneeler

A screen or partition to be placed between the chair and kneeler

Props:
Bell for Father Hearn to ring

Small white purse for Molly

Costumes:
Priest's collar, black jacket, black pants for Father Hearn

Catholic school uniform for Molly

THE NOIR BEFORE CHRISTMAS

JOHN MINIGAN

Reprinted by permission of the author.

For performance rights, contact John Minigan, john.a.minigan@gmail.com

Synopsis
On Christmas Eve, Mary Claus brings private detective (and former elf) Jack Frost a missing persons case. Who's missing? The Fat Man himself. Can Jack find Santa and save Christmas? Will his ex-lover Rudee learn to lay off the peppermint schnapps before her nose goes permanently red? Will Jack learn not to give up so easily? And what about love? Tough questions, all. But at Christmas, there's only one way to answer.

Time
Christmas Eve

Characters

JACK FROST, male-presenting, 20s-50s, an elf and private detective formerly employed at Santa's Workshop

MARY CLAUS, female-presenting, 20s-50s, Jack's ex, now married to The Fat Man

RUDEE, female-presenting, 20s-40s, a dancer, her nose may be bright, but her past sure wasn't

THE FAT MAN, male-presenting, 20s-50s, Santa himself

Note: One actor can play Mary and Rudee, and maybe even The Fat Man.

Settings
Jack's office near the North Pole, with a desk and two chairs.
The Little Drummer Boy, a strip club and bar with two bar stools.

Estimated run time
10 minutes

THE NOIR BEFORE CHRISTMAS

[Note: Line breaks are intentional and reflect the rhythm of the dialogue.] A sax plays something sultry and Christmas-y.

Lights reveal JACK FROST, a little guy who has traded in his elf hat for a trilby, a trench coat, and too much time in a dingy office near the North Pole.

JACK speaks to us directly.

JACK
It was Christmas Eve, the one-year anniversary of the night I quit my elf gig in Santa's Workshop, tired of the grind, tired of livin' in a fog of hot cocoa and gingerbread. But mostly? Tired of the guy who'd taken so much away from me: The Fat Man himself. People always said I gave up too easy, but the way things had gone with me and Old Nick, I saw no reason to stick all the way to twelve drummers drummin'. So I struck out on my own as Jack Frost, the North Pole's one and only private dick.
How'd that work out for me? Like the wise guy said, " 'twas the night before Christmas and nothin' was stirrin'."

There's a knock on a door just off stage.

Or at least it was nothin' till my ex-lover came a-wassailin'.

JACK pushes a button on his desk, and we hear a buzzer.

MARY CLAUS comes in, dressed in a festive red suit and dark sunglasses.

Well, well, well. If it ain't Mary Christmas.

MARY
It's Mary Claus now, Jack. You know that.

JACK
Yeah, Santa's got his Claus all over you these days. What are you doin' here on Christmas Eve?

MARY
I got no place else to turn.

JACK
(narrating)
Life with The Fat Man had changed Mary. She was still a beauty, but one look told you that all was not calm, and all was not bright.
(*to MARY*) What's the matter, kid?

MARY
It's Santa. He's gone.

JACK
On Christmas Eve? He's probably right down Santa Claus Lane.

MARY
That's the first place I looked.

JACK
Then he's dashin' through the snow!

MARY
The sleigh's still in the garage! I'm worried sick, Jack. If he doesn't come back, it's the end of Christmas for everybody!

JACK
Would that be so bad? My life's been better with no Santa in it.

MARY
It's better, is it? Look at ya. All alone in your office on Christmas Eve.

JACK
(narrating)
Maybe she was right. Life after Santa's Workshop was lonely, and my bells hadn't been jingled in a long time.
(*to MARY*) I'm not alone now that you're here, doll.

MARY

Don't call me that. What have ya got to calm my nerves?

JACK

The usual?

MARY nods. JACK pours eggnog into two shot glasses.

Have a seat. And take off the cheaters, will ya? We ain't seen the sun in a long time, you and me.

MARY takes off her sunglasses.

Nutmeg?

MARY

Oh, Jack. You remember.

JACK

I remember a lot of things, kid. A lot of nights that weren't so holy. Nights I've been tryin' to forget.
Glad tidings.

JACK and MARY clink glasses and drink.

It seems you're in the market for a shamus to find The Fat Man. Any ideas where he might have gone?

MARY

I wouldn't know where to look, but I know who to ask.

JACK

Whom.

MARY

Whom. If anybody's out to get Santa, it'd be her. I think you should talk to her. You gotta save Christmas, Jack. Think of the children. Visions of sugar plums shattered like so many dropped candy canes.

JACK
The sooner they learn life's no winter wonderland, the better off they'll be.

MARY
If ya won't do it for the children, then do it for me. If ya still care.

JACK
Ya know I care, Mary.

> *JACK takes MARY in his arms.*

But suppose I can't find him? Suppose he's really gone? Any chance you'll let our love light gleam again?

> *JACK holds a sprig of mistletoe over MARY.*

MARY
Oh, Jack. Don't.

JACK
If that's the way ya want it.

> *JACK pockets the mistletoe and releases MARY.*

MARY
Just find him. Please.

JACK
All right, kid. For "Auld Lang Syne."

> *A sax again plays a sultry Christmas-y song. MARY leaves, and JACK pours and drinks another shot of eggnog while he addresses us directly.*

Gettin' Mary back together with The Fat Man was an item I'd left off my Christmas list, but the holidays looked a little more festive when I had a case to work — even a missing persons. And Mary was right: If I was going to find Nick, there was somebody I had to talk to first. Somebody who'd lost her own gig with him right around the time I walked away from mine. Somebody who'd been tryin' to get herself clean when The Fat Man let her go. Now, I heard she was back to drownin' her sorrows in peppermint schnapps. And she was back to dancin' — pole dancin' — North Pole dancin' — at a joint called The Little Drummer Boy. But I reckon I was partly to blame for that. Anyway, that's where I found her, sittin' alone at the bar after her shift. Her hair was the same bright red I remembered, and — I guess she was back on the joy juice after all — so was her nose.

We see RUDEE, in antlers, flaming red hair, and, once she turns to see us, a red nose, too. We're in The Little Drummer Boy, and she's working her way through a bottle of peppermint schnapps.

Evenin', Rudee.

RUDEE
Well, if it ain't Jack Frost. How ya been, lover?

JACK
Fulla comfort and joy, Red, same as always. I figured I'd find ya here.

RUDEE
Nice to know somebody's lookin'. I hear ya walked away from the elf gig. What are ya doin' with yourself these days, sittin' on a shelf like the rest of 'em?

JACK
Private dick.

RUDEE
Traded the jingle boots for a pair of gumshoes, didja?

JACK
And I got a question for ya.

RUDEE
So it's business, not pleasure. What a shame.

JACK
The Fat Man's missin'.

RUDEE
On Christmas Eve?

JACK
You wouldn't happen to know anything about that, would ya? Personally?

RUDEE
After the way he treated me — plyin' me with schnapps to keep my nose so bright and not includin' rehab in the health plan? Sure, I wouldn't mind seeing the big guy's chestnuts roasting on an open fire, but I don't have a vindictive antler on my body. If I did hold a grudge, would I be talkin' to you?

JACK
I know, Red. I'm sorry about the way things ended for us.

RUDEE
The Fat Man had no use for me when I was clean, and you had no use for me when I wasn't. I thought we might end up back together someday, but maybe you're always gonna be my missing person.

JACK
I got tired of your reindeer games, Red!

RUDEE
Truth is, I was never good enough for ya. Or for him. Or any of 'em. The way they'd laugh and call me names. I guess the truth is, I'm no good for anybody! Not even myself!

JACK
Come on, Red. You got clean once, you can do it again.

RUDEE
And lose the one thing guys like Nick are willing to pay for? No, with me it looks like the lantern's always gonna match the drapes. Nice seein' ya, Jack. Makes me think about what coulda been.

JACK

See ya in the funny papers, Red.

> *JACK starts to go.*

RUDEE

You know your problem, lover? You always give up too easy.

JACK

Is that so?

RUDEE

Look, I don't know where Nick went, but if he left Mary, there's one place I'd look first. I imagine ya know where that is. And with who.

JACK

Whom.

RUDEE

Whom.

JACK

You tellin' me he's with… Vixen?

RUDEE

Always trust where your mind goes first, Jack. I'd lay even money that's where Nick's mind went, too.

JACK

I appreciate the tip, Red. Here.

> *JACK gives her a gold foil-wrapped chocolate.*

RUDEE

Thanks, Jack. I'd keep this next to my heart, but I wouldn't want <u>it</u> to melt, too.

> *A sax plays as JACK comes forward to address us.*

JACK

There are things that go on north of the Arctic Circle that civilians to the south never know. Things like travel routes, or how many cc's of insulin a Fat Man needs for half a billion plates of cookies. But there was more. Things that happen when the night is six months long and nobody can make more than one walk of shame a year. Rudee had pointed her pretty pink proboscis in the path of Santa's sultriest sleigh scooter, Vixen. Suddenly, it all made sense, and I had a pretty good idea what to do. Droppin' the dime on Santa and Vixen could cause enough chaos to clamp the kibosh on Christmas for every kid in creation, but it might also bring Mary Christmas back into my life. And maybe that was good enough for me.
Back in the office as the midnight clear approached, I was about call Mary to give her the news when a familiar shadow filled my office doorway.

The shadow appears and THE FAT MAN enters, carrying a large satchel, holding it up as if pointing a concealed gun at JACK.

THE FAT MAN

Evenin', Jack.

JACK

Well, if it ain't jolly old St. Nicholas.

JACK raises his hands.

THE FAT MAN

I understand ya been looking for me.

JACK

Who peached? Rudee?

THE FAT MAN

Ya think I don't know what ya been up to? I see ya when you're sleepin', see? I know when you're awake —

JACK

All right, I get it. But Santa takin' a powder on Christmas Eve? Mary asked me to give your whereabouts the up-and-down. She's been worried about ya.

THE NOIR BEFORE CHRISTMAS

THE FAT MAN
I know that, too.

JACK
And she's worried about a couple billion kids waking up without so much as a lump of coal in their stocking.

THE FAT MAN
I'll get to 'em. Don't worry.

JACK
Go on and shoot me if that's what ya want, but at least tell me where ya been.

JACK lowers his arms.

And with who.

THE FAT MAN
(threatening)

Whom!

JACK raises his arms back up.

JACK
Whom! It was Vixen, wasn't it?

THE FAT MAN
You heard that from Rudee, didn't ya. I can't pretend I ain't been tempted.

He lowers the bag and JACK lowers his arms.

Long, lonely sleigh rides with nothing but moonlight and the sound of sleigh bells, starin' at the sleek haunches of an octet of concupiscent caribou sexpots? Sure, I' been tempted! But I ain't never strayed. Mary's the only one for me.

JACK
I see.

THE FAT MAN
I know that's a disappointment. I know how ya feel about her.

JACK
How do you know that?

THE FAT MAN
'Cause I know if ya been bad or good.

JACK
I' been good, for goodness' sake. So what am I supposed to tell Mary?

THE FAT MAN
The truth.

JACK
I used to think I knew what that was. I used to think the truth was that Santa's a giver. But you take. And it looks like you're trying to take joy from the world like ya took Mary Christmas away from me.

THE FAT MAN
I didn't take her, Jack. She chose me 'cause I was jolly in ways you could never be. Mary and me? We're the holly and the ivy.

JACK
Then I don't get it. If ya still love her, why'd ya run away?

THE FAT MAN
'Tis the season.

JACK
What's that supposed to mean?

THE FAT MAN
I am a giver, Jack, not a taker. It's the season for gifts, and I got one for <u>you</u>, right here.

JACK
What?

THE FAT MAN again holds the bag up like he's pointing a gun, and JACK puts his hands back up. But THE FAT MAN pulls the bag away, and we see he's holding a coffee carafe or pot. It would be awesome if it were somehow magically full of hot, steaming coffee. But you might also use a simple percolator.

I don't understand.

THE FAT MAN

It's just part of what I got in store. Here.

THE FAT MAN hands the carafe over to JACK.

JACK

I still don't get it.

THE FAT MAN

No? Maybe this'll clear things up.

He takes out a bottle of peppermint syrup.

JACK

Peppermint syrup?

THE FAT MAN

I asked Mary to tell ya I was missin', and that there was somebody you should talk to.

JACK

She told me to go to Rudee.

THE FAT MAN

Did she tell you that? Or was Rudee the first thought in your head? Like she told ya, always trust where your mind goes first.

JACK

How do you know what Rudee said to me?

THE FAT MAN

Jack, we've been over this!
Go to her. Get her to trade in the schnapps for a hot mug o' joe with a shot of this sweet, minty holiday joy. Alcohol-free.

JACK takes the bottle of peppermint syrup.

You know she'll listen to ya.

JACK

Are you doing this just to make me forget about Mary?

THE FAT MAN

I'm doing this because you need to stop giving up so easy. I'm doing this because if Rudee's got you and you got her, maybe you both got a chance to be merry and bright in this cockamamie world.

JACK

Why do you care about any of that?

THE FAT MAN

I got one reason and one reason only:

A la "I'm Batman."

I'm Santa Claus.

THE FAT MAN goes to the exit and turns.

Merry Christmas, Jack.

THE FAT MAN leaves. Somewhere, a distant saxophone starts to play, a sultry but cheerful Christmas-y song.

JACK
(narrating)

Turns out, the big guy was right. You should never give up easy. Not on anything, not on anyone. And always trust where your mind goes first. 'Cause when the nights are as long and dark and cold as they are in these parts, ya don't want 'em to be silent. It's a whole lot better when your sleigh bells are jinglin'. Ring ting tinglin', too.

RUDEE comes in, her nose no longer red. She's holding two holiday mugs. She hands one to JACK.

Cuppa joe, kid?

RUDEE

Please do.

JACK pours some coffee for RUDEE, then for himself.

JACK

Here you go, Red.

RUDEE

How'd ya like to slip me some of your sweet holiday cheer tonight, lover?

JACK

All that caffeine at this hour? Maybe tonight, we can make it a double.

JACK pours two shots of peppermint syrup into RUDEE's mug, then turns to address us directly.

Mary came to me that night to warn me it might be the end of Christmas. But when it came to Rudee and me, it was the start of the most wonderful time of the year.

JACK and RUDEE clink mugs. JACK pulls out more mistletoe, holds it over them. They kiss.

The saxophone blows a happy Christmas-y tune.

END OF PLAY

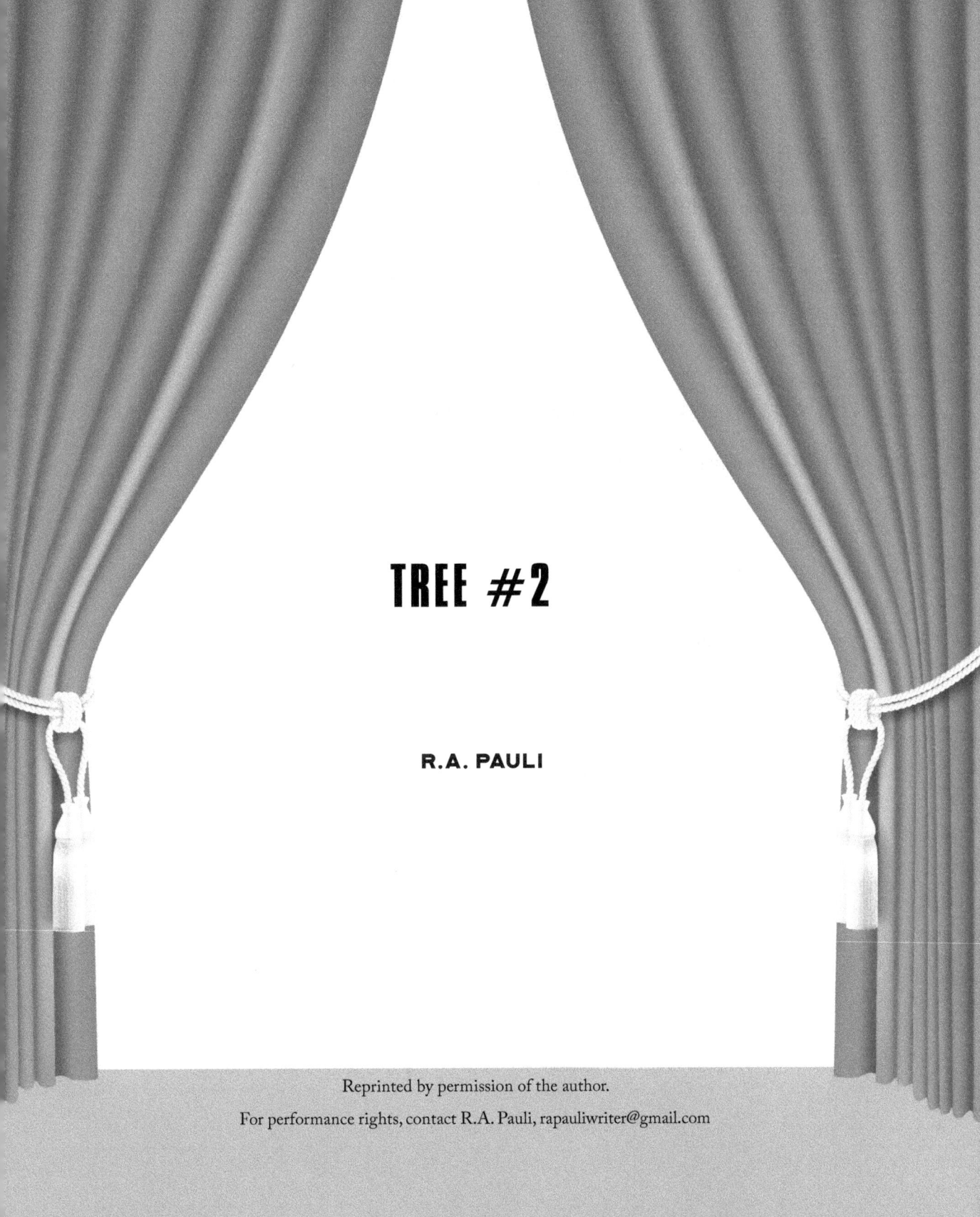

TREE #2

R.A. PAULI

Reprinted by permission of the author.
For performance rights, contact R.A. Pauli, rapauliwriter@gmail.com

Synopsis
Charlie is having trouble understanding his character's motivation. He has questions for his director. So many questions. Perhaps one too many?

Time
Present day

Characters
DIRECTOR, any gender, any age, any ethnicity

CHARLIE, any gender, any age, any ethnicity

Setting
A community theater rehearsal space

Estimated run time
10 minutes

TREE #2

At rise, we see DIRECTOR, looking at the script while speaking to the invisible cast members of a play being rehearsed.

DIRECTOR

Okay, everyone, moving on. In this scene, our hero Jack is approaching the giant beanstalk that's miraculously sprouted from his magic beans —

CHARLIE

Offstage.

Excuse me!

DIRECTOR

Looking up, partly surprised, partly irritated by the interruption.

What?!

CHARLIE

Enters, approaches DIRECTOR.

Excuse me, sorry to interrupt, but —

DIRECTOR

Are you in this scene?

CHARLIE

Yes, I am.

DIRECTOR

You're late. Please find your mark as quickly as —

CHARLIE

Well, but here's the thing —

DIRECTOR
Just please take your place so we can get started —

CHARLIE
But —

DIRECTOR
Is there a problem? Don't you know where your mark is?

CHARLIE
Of course, I know where my mark is.

DIRECTOR
Okay, good, so just go there —

CHARLIE
What I don't know is what my motivation is in this scene.

DIRECTOR
Your motivation?

CHARLIE
Right. Why am I doing what I'm doing?

DIRECTOR
(Flips a couple pages in the script.)

Sorry, who are you?

CHARLIE
I'm Charlie.

DIRECTOR
(Studying page)
Charlie… Charlie… And you're playing…?

TREE #2

CHARLIE
(proudly)

Tree Number Two!

DIRECTOR
(Pause. Can't believe this.)

Tree Number Two?!

CHARLIE

Correct.

DIRECTOR

And you want to know what your motivation is?

CHARLIE

Yes! What am I doing? Why am I doing it?

DIRECTOR

You're a tree. Your motivation is to be a tree. Your action is to stand very still, think tree-ish thoughts, and project tree-ness to the best of your ability as an actor.

CHARLIE

But what sort of tree am I?

DIRECTOR

It doesn't matter.

CHARLIE

So, you're saying that an elm tree would have the same thoughts as a willow tree or an oak tree?

DIRECTOR

As far as I know, yes.

CHARLIE

I find that highly unlikely.

DIRECTOR
Uh-huh. Okay, Charlie, look. You're a generic tree. Just stand still and think generic tree thoughts.

CHARLIE
But shouldn't I be the same kind of tree as Tree Number One? I mean, wouldn't, like, a Sequoia standing next to a Japanese Maple tax an audience's suspension of disbelief?

DIRECTOR
I doubt it, but if it makes you feel better, then fine, be the same sort of tree as Tree Number One.

CHARLIE
Okay, great! (*pause*)
So, what sort of tree is Tree Number One?

DIRECTOR
(irritated, losing patience)
Oh, for the love of —! Tree Number One is a GENERIC TREE! Just. Like. YOU! Okay? Are we good? Can we get on with —?

CHARLIE
(oblivious)
Do you think Tree Number Two is jealous of Tree Number One? Maybe there's lingering sapling rivalry? Or… or even an Oedipal complex festering beneath the seemingly placid leafy surface?

DIRECTOR
Listen carefully, Charlie. There is no sapling rivalry. There is no Oedipal complex. Tree Number Two has nothing on its mind. Tree Number Two is simply standing still, being in the moment, oblivious to everything else.

CHARLIE
(contemplates this briefly)
But why should Tree Number Two be standing still? What if there's a breeze?

TREE #2

DIRECTOR

There is no breeze.

CHARLIE

How do you know?

DIRECTOR

I'm the director. It's my job to know. Trust me. There is no breeze.

CHARLIE

Wouldn't a breeze be more interesting? Get some movement into the scene?

Throws arms over his head, starts swaying while making wooshing noises, to demonstrate.

DIRECTOR

The audience is watching Jack climb a beanstalk. That's enough movement. We don't need swaying trees to distract from the main action.

CHARLIE
(stops swaying, presses his argument)

It's not a distraction, it's an <u>enhancement</u>! It could be a gale, even, or a raging thunderstorm, imperiling Jack's climb! Tree Number One could be <u>uprooted</u>!

DIRECTOR

No.

CHARLIE

No?

DIRECTOR

No breeze. No gale. No thunderstorm. No uprooting. To summarize — no.

CHARLIE

But if Tree Number One were uprooted, Tree Number Two could come to its rescue!

DIRECTOR
This scene is not about a gallant tree rescue. The trees are not the focus, okay?

CHARLIE
So, you're telling me the trees don't matter in this play?

DIRECTOR
The <u>beanstalk</u> is what matters. The trees? Beanstalk sidekicks, at best.

Looks at watch.

Okay, listen, we really have to move on.

CHARLIE
Sidekicks! Trees are the lungs of our planet! Without trees, we'd all suffocate!

DIRECTOR
Look, Charlie —

CHARLIE
It's not <u>beanstalks</u> that keep people alive — it's <u>trees</u>!

DIRECTOR
That's all well and good. Hooray for trees. I promise to hug the first tree I see after this rehearsal. But our play is "Jack and the <u>Beanstalk</u>," not "Jack and the <u>Tree</u>"! So —

CHARLIE
It's a miracle that Tree Number Two exists at all! Tree Number Two probably had to overcome drought and poor soil and foraging birds and insects and fungus, fiercely struggling to gain a precarious roothold and survive to become a… a fine generic tree. We should be doing a play about <u>that</u>, not a stupid <u>fairy tale</u>!

DIRECTOR
That's a great backstory for Tree Number Two, Charlie.

CHARLIE
It is?

DIRECTOR
Absolutely! Use it while you're standing <u>very still</u>, projecting your best immobile tree vibe.

CHARLIE
Use it?

DIRECTOR
Think of the suffering, the uncertainty, the desperation of the ordeal you've been through. Think of how incredibly <u>tired</u> that's made you. Incapable of stirring even a <u>single leaf</u>. And yet —

CHARLIE
And yet our intrepid Tree Number Two resolutely holds fast, canopy striking a noble pose, silhouetted against a threatening sky as Jack, scrambling up the mysterious, magical beanstalk, pauses for a moment to give a jaunty wave to his faithful forest friend —

DIRECTOR
Um, well —

CHARLIE
— then continues his perilous ascent, secure in the knowledge that Tree Number Two has his back! Now I get it!

DIRECTOR
You do?

CHARLIE
Yes! Theatre is a collaborative art. No part is insignificant, right? So it's up to each and every actor to give his or her utmost to help make the play succeed.

DIRECTOR
(nodding head in appreciation and relief)
Well said, Charlie. I think you <u>do</u> get it!

CHARLIE
Thanks.

DIRECTOR
Good, that's settled. Shall we get to rehearsing now? Are you ready?

CHARLIE
I sure am!

DIRECTOR
That's the spirit!

CHARLIE
(looking around)
Uh… where is everyone?

DIRECTOR
(checking watch)
Our stage manager probably told everyone to take ten while we finished our conversation. They should be right back.

CHARLIE
Oh, okay.

DIRECTOR
So if you need a bathroom break, now would be the time —

CHARLIE
Actually, I have another question.

DIRECTOR
(a bit leery)
I thought we'd settled everything about Tree Number Two.

CHARLIE
Oh yes, we have. I completely understand what Tree Number Two has to do.

TREE #2

DIRECTOR
Ah, okay, that's great! So then, what's your question?

CHARLIE
(after a beat)
Why didn't you cast me as Tree Number One?

Blackout.

END OF PLAY

YOUR CALL IS IMPORTANT TO US

JANET R. CARPMAN

Reprinted by permission of the author.
For performance rights, contact Janet R. Carpman, jcarpman@comcast.net

COMEDIES FOR THE VIRTUAL STAGE

Synopsis
Cassie, a woman working from home during the pandemic, repeatedly calls tech support at her Wi-Fi company to solve a critical problem. Thwarted at every turn, she eventually lands on an unexpected solution.

Time
2020, during the COVID-19 pandemic

Characters
CASSIE, female, 50+, high-strung, working from home

RECORDING, male, 45+, resonant voice, as in an infomercial

PHONE TECHS #1, #2, #3, #5, 25+, any gender

PHONE TECH #4, offshore worker, 25+, any gender, speaks English with an accent

HOME TECH, male, 55+, easygoing

Settings
CASSIE'S messy home office

PHONE TECHS #1, #2, #3, #4, #5 makeshift home offices

CASSIE'S living room, with a door to the kitchen

CASSIE'S home office, neat and organized

Estimated run time
20 minutes

YOUR CALL IS IMPORTANT TO US

Working from home, CASSIE sits at her desk, typing on a keyboard. She can't do what she wants to do. She makes a face, shakes her head, and tries a second time. Again, she is thwarted. She picks up her cell phone and dials.

RECORDING
(fake-friendly)

Welcome to WiFi4U! Your call is important to us. To ensure quality, this call may be monitored or recorded. To learn more about our privacy practices, please visit us at WiFi4U dot com, forward slash, privacy, underscore, practices. Thanks for calling, (*beat*) CASSIE. Give me a few seconds to review your account.

SFX Keyboard keys clicking

All done! As you may be aware, many of our agents are working from home now, due to COVID-19, so it will take them longer than usual to respond. We appreciate your patience! In a few words, tell me how WiFi4U can serve you today.

CASSIE
(matter-of-factly)

The paste function in my email doesn't work.

RECORDING

Please be aware that our menu options have changed. You can press 1 or say, "Main Menu," press 2 or say "Password Reset," press 3 or say "Tech Support."

CASSIE

Tech Support.

RECORDING

We are busy assisting other customers. Your call will be answered in the order in which it was received. Please hold while we transfer you to a customer care representative. Your estimated hold time is 20-30 minutes. You can listen to your choice of music while you wait. Which of the following would you prefer: Jazz, R&B, Country, Classical, or Show Tunes?

CASSIE

Jazz

SFX Twangy country music

PHONE TECH #1
(chirpy)
Hello! It's a beautiful day here at WiFi4U! This is Jamie, your personal tech support manager. Whom do I have the pleasure of speaking with?

CASSIE
What? (*beat*) Oh, you want my name?

PHONE TECH #1
Yes, please, ma'am.

CASSIE
Cassie.

PHONE TECH #1
How do you spell that? (*slowly*) K as in Kilo, A as in Alpha, T as in Tango, H as in Hotel, and Y as in Yankee?

CASSIE
(annoyed)
No! Not Kathy, Cassie!

PHONE TECH #1
Oh, I get it! (*slowly*) K as in Kilo, A as in Alpha, T as in…

CASSIE
(cutting them off, resigned)
Close enough.

PHONE TECH #1
So hello, Katie! How is your day going so far?

CASSIE
(surprised, but plays along)
What? (*two beats*) Well, I was doing fine until I took my laundry out of the machine this morning and discovered — so stupid — that I had washed my red bandana with my black and white bedspread, which was now PINK! (*lowers voice, slightly abashed*) Oh, you were just being polite?

YOUR CALL IS IMPORTANT TO US

PHONE TECH #1
(still chirpy)
We are always interested in our customers! So, how can I help you today?

CASSIE
I'm having trouble with the paste function in my emails.

PHONE TECH #1
What?

CASSIE
The paste function.

PHONE TECH #1
Did you say the chaste function? (*lewdly*) My, my!

CASSIE
No! The paste function.

PHONE TECH #1
The waste function?

CASSIE
No! (*into the phone*) Paste: P-A-S-T-E

PHONE TECH #1
(huffy) Please spell it using the telephone alphabet, as I did.

CASSIE
(fed up)
Very well. P as in… Pardon me, but this is absurd, A as in… Asinine, S as in… Shoot me now, T as in…

PHONE TECH #1
(annoyed, cutting her off)
Oh! Pasta!

CASSIE
No! Paste!

PHONE TECH #1
Sorry, there's no pasta function on our platform. *(leans in)* And, in all honesty, I'm feeling some serious negativity from you, ma'am, so I'll have to let you go now. Have a nice day!

CASSIE stands up and calls Tech Support again. SFX dial tone, outgoing call ringing, click

RECORDING
Welcome to WiFi4U! Your call is important to us. Your call may be recorded for training and quality purposes. I see you just called a short while ago *(beat)* CASSIE! Before we get started, please be aware that our menu options have changed.

CASSIE
(flabbergasted)

In just the last few minutes?

RECORDING
Please let us know if you, yourself, are exhibiting any of the symptoms of COVID-19. Press 1 or say "Fever or chills," press 2 or say "Cough," press 3 or say "Shortness of breath," press 4 or say "New loss of taste or smell," press 5 or say "None of the above."

CASSIE
(rolling her eyes, weirded out)

Uh… None of the above.

RECORDING
That's good! Your health is important to us. Please maintain the recommended social distance between you and your phone. Now, why are you calling back again so soon? Did you change your mind? Do you have another problem? Do you want to wait on hold some more? Do you just looove the sound of my voice? Or something else?

CASSIE
Something else.

YOUR CALL IS IMPORTANT TO US

> RECORDING

Give me a few seconds to review your account.

SFX Keyboard keys clicking

> RECORDING

All done! In a few words, tell me how WiFi4U can serve you today.

> CASSIE

The paste function in my email doesn't work, and it's really important because I have to...

> RECORDING
> (cutting her off)

That's what you called about before! Didn't you get it fixed by now?

> CASSIE

No!

> RECORDING

You can say, "Your last agent didn't do their job," "This Wi-Fi is not really for ME," or "Tech support."

> CASSIE
> (reluctant to say what is really on her mind)

Um... Tech support.

> RECORDING

Please hold while we transfer you to a customer care representative. And, for goodness' sake, don't make a fuss if they can't help you! They're trying their best. Not everyone is as perfect as you! Your call may be answered in the order it was received, or it may not be, depending... Your estimated hold time is 60-90 minutes. You can listen to your choice of music while you wait.
Which of the following would you prefer: Jazz, R&B, Country, Classical, or Show Tunes?

CASSIE
Mmm... R&B.

SFX: very fast classical music

PHONE TECH #2
Hello! It's a beautiful day here at WiFi4U! This is Taylor, your confidential tech support manager. Whom do I have the pleasure of speaking with?

CASSIE
My name is Cassie, and I've just been hung up on and have had to wait on hold for what seemed like years. Can you help me?

PHONE TECH #2
Of course, ma'am! Let me first verify your identity. What is your Social Security number?

CASSIE
What? (*beat*) I thought you're never supposed to give that out.

PHONE TECH #2
Well then, (*hesitates*) just tell it to me in reverse.

CASSIE
In reverse? Uh, (*says the number to herself*) 8... 2... 5... Sorry, brain freeze.

PHONE TECH #2
Okay. Let's try this instead: (*slowly*) What was the day of the week, date, month, year, and time — using the 24-hour clock — in hours, minutes, and seconds, of your first-ever call to WiFi4U Tech Support?

CASSIE
(taken aback)
You're kidding! I have no idea! Uh, (*several beats*) 2002?

PHONE TECH #2
Never mind. What is the problem, ma'am?

YOUR CALL IS IMPORTANT TO US

CASSIE
The paste function doesn't work in my emails, and I have to use it or else I…

PHONE TECH #2
(cutting her off)
The baste function? Maybe you need a cooking app.

CASSIE
Noooo. (*impatiently*) Let me speak to a supervisor. But first, please be sure I don't have to wait on hold again and that you've documented my call.

PHONE TECH #2
(annoyed)
No problem, ma'am. I'll escalate the call.

CASSIE
And please don't call me ma'am.

PHONE TECH #2
Yes, ma'am. Transferring you now…

CASSIE starts pacing

PHONE TECH #3 picks up

PHONE TECH #3
Hello. This is WiFi4U supervisor number 3-9-1-0-1-7-7-2-0-0-0-8-7-7-9-8 in escalation. How can I help you?

CASSIE
The paste function won't work when I use email on my computer, and I need it, because if I can't…

PHONE TECH #3
(cutting her off)
Mm hmm.

PHONE TECH #3 types loudly on a keyboard.

Hmmm. Okay. Uh-huh. I see. Yup. Got it. Cool! Just a few questions to verify your identity, and we'll get started.

CASSIE
(Dubious)

Okay.

PHONE TECH #3
(Fast but clear)

What brand of computer do you have? When and where did you purchase it? How much did you pay? Did you look for a better deal elsewhere? Did you pay with cash or credit card? What is your CVV number? What operating system do you use? When was the last time you backed up? What programs do you use most often? How do you keep track of your passwords? What is your favorite color? What is your blood type? Do you own a selfie stick? When did you last buy a lottery ticket? Any fun facts you'd like to share?

CASSIE

Wait! What???

PHONE TECH #3

Just want to be sure we know everything about you, ma'am. Your call is important to us!

CASSIE

PLEASE! Just help me with my issue!

PHONE TECH #3

Your magazine issue?

CASSIE

Nooooo. My email issue. Remember?

PHONE TECH #3

What was it again?

YOUR CALL IS IMPORTANT TO US

CASSIE
(leading them, helping them remember)
The PASTE function…

PHONE TECH #3
Oh, right.

Leans in to speak confidentially

You see, ma'am, I just started working here. Actually, it's my first day.

CASSIE
Oh no! Can you please connect me with an experienced supervisor?

PHONE TECH #3
(good-naturedly)
Okay. I'll escalate the call.

CASSIE
But — that's how I got to YOU.

PHONE TECH #3
(cheerfully, after a beat or two)
Then, I'll just elevate the escalation!

CASSIE
(exhales with exasperation)
And make sure they get all the notes, so I don't have to repeat everything. And please, please don't make me wait on hold again.

PHONE TECH #3
Of course not, ma'am! Have a wonderful day! Transferring you now.

CASSIE takes out her knitting and angrily starts to knit

RECORDING
We're pleased to offer your choice of music: Oldies or (beat) Oldies!

SFX music – annoying Oldies hit

SFX international call static

PHONE TECH #4 in an offshore, makeshift office, answers. Speaks English with an accent.

PHONE TECH #4
Hello? This is WiFi4U supervisor number 9-0-8-4-9-3-2-6-1-8-3-7-4-9-5-5 in elevated, escalated tech support, speaking on a recorded line. What seems to be the problem?

CASSIE
Do you have the notes from my last two calls?

PHONE TECH #4
What about boats?

CASSIE
No, not boats, NOTES.

PHONE TECH #4
Musical notes?

CASSIE
Noooo. Do you have the notes from my previous calls?

SFX rooster crows

PHONE TECH #4
No, I see nothing in the record.

CASSIE
(under her breath)
Oh my friggin god…

YOUR CALL IS IMPORTANT TO US

PHONE TECH #4
Let's get started! I'll just ask you a few questions to verify your identity. Okay, ma'am? Here we go!

CASSIE
(sensing doom)

Oh no!

PHONE TECH #4
(fast but clear)

What's your address? How long have you lived there? Where did you live before that? And before that? What was the first telephone number you had as a child? What was your second grade teacher's name? Do you have a dog? What is its name? Are you gluten-intolerant? What was the name of your high school? What was your class rank? Your SAT score? Do you still have your tonsils? Who is your bestie? Do you consider yourself a Democrat, Republican, Independent, Green Party, or none of the above?

CASSIE
(starts whimpering)

Whaaaaat??

PHONE TECH #4
Never mind. Please describe the problem in eight words or less. Extra credit for exactly eight!

CASSIE
(still whimpering) The paste function in my email doesn't work.

PHONE TECH #4 counts the words on his fingers.

PHONE TECH #4
Good for you! Extra credit!

(*Fast, but clear*) When did you first notice the problem? What times of day does it occur? Does it depend on what you're wearing? Does it depend on who the email is going to? How frustrating is this on a scale of 1 to 100, where 1 is not frustrating at all and 100 is so frustrating you're going to scream?

CASSIE
(yelling into the phone)
You don't understand! I have a work deadline, and if I don't get this fixed, I'll...

PHONE TECH #4
(cutting her off, speaking slowly)
I hear you! Just be patient, ma'am. I can DEFINITELY help you with this problem. No worries. First, please unplug everything: your modem and router, every connection to your computer, your printer, and every other connection.

CASSIE

Whyyyyy?

PHONE TECH #4
We want to start again with a completely virgin system. Okay? You're doing this?

CASSIE
(resigned)
Oh... kay... Give me some time.

PHONE TECH #4
No problem! I'll wait! I'll just eat my breakfast.

PHONE TECH #4 eats crunchy cereal out of a bowl with a spoon.

CASSIE moves around her office to the various pieces of equipment, gets on her hands and knees to peer behind the computer, and starts pulling out plugs, cords, and wires, grunting as she does this.

SFX rooster crows

CASSIE sits up.

CASSIE
(out of breath)
Is that a real rooster I've been hearing?

YOUR CALL IS IMPORTANT TO US

PHONE TECH #4
(giggling)
Yes ma'am. I apologize. I can't do anything about it. It belongs to my neighbor. I'm so sorry.

CASSIE
(giggling)
That's Okay. It's just so… weird!
(*Big exhale*) Okay, now everything's unplugged.

PHONE TECH #4
Good! Wait ten minutes. I'll just drink my tea.

CASSIE puts her head down on her desk.

PHONE TECH #4 slurps tea from a mug.

A slow count of four.

PHONE TECH #4
Time's up! Okay! Now reconnect and plug everything back in!

Once again, CASSIE moves around her office, gets on her hands and knees to peer behind the computer, and starts putting back plugs, cords, and wires, grunting as she does this.

A slow count of eight.

PHONE TECH #4
Tell me what's happening, ma'am! Are you all set?

CASSIE
Not quite. I had to figure out what went where, but I think I did it. Now, give me a minute…

CASSIE sits down at her desk and prays that it will work.

SFX keyboard keys clicking

CASSIE
(horrified)

Oh my god! My programs are GONE! My settings have disappeared! Where is my dayta, uh, datta? OH NO!!!

PHONE TECH #4

No worries! Just reinstall, reset, and re-enter everything, then call us back. Have I solved your problem?

SFX rooster crows

(Use a sign or a slide that indicates "One Week Later")

CASSIE calls Tech Support, yet again.

SFX dial tone, outgoing call ringing, click

RECORDING
(snarkily)

Welcome to WiFi4U! Your call is important to us, but we suspect WE aren't very important to YOU, (*beat*) CASSIE! Why, even though we can't see you, we know you're out there rolling your eyes at us. This call may be monitored or recorded, so we'll know if you get angry and swear at our customer care representatives. (*frighteningly*) In that case, we'll put you in "on-hold hell" for days at a time. (*fake pleasant*) So, in a few words, tell me how WiFi4U can serve you today.

CASSIE
(gritting her teeth)

The paste function in my email STILL doesn't work. I can't complete my project without it, and I'm really afraid I'll get…

RECORDING
(interrupts her, more snark)

I see. We're experiencing high call volume, but we want you to know that our representatives are working hard to answer your call. Your estimated hold time is 4-6 hours. Yes! You heard that right. You can listen to your choice of music while you wait. Which of the following would you prefer: Jazz, R&B, Country, Classical, or Show Tunes?

YOUR CALL IS IMPORTANT TO US

CASSIE
(yelling)

Just silence, please!

SFX corny Christmas music

CASSIE starts sobbing.

PHONE TECH #5
(Softly hums and bops to the music)

Hello! It's a beautiful day here at WiFi4U! This is Frankie, your wellness tech support manager. Whom do I have the pleasure of speaking with?

CASSIE
(sobbing)

You have to help me!

PHONE TECH #5

Please calm yourself, ma'am. Try a few cleansing breaths.

Breathes visibly and audibly, in and out, two times. CASSIE joins in on #2.

Better? Okay! Let's get started! First, I need to confirm your identity!

CASSIE

Nooooo.

PHONE TECH #5
(calmly)

Breathe in, breathe out… Breathe in, breathe out…

CASSIE joins in for the second breath.

PHONE TECH #5

Good! Ready? Go!

CASSIE
(fast but clear)

Cassie Cassidy, 5-6-3-1 McDonald Avenue, 6-1-7-5-5-5-8-4-8-8, PC, desktop, Windows Ten, favorite color: teal, a dog named CJ, buy Lottery tickets every other week, second-grade teacher's name: Mrs. Morgan. Blood type: A positive. Fun fact: played the trombone in the high school marching band.

PHONE TECH #5
(slowly)

Hmmm. Let me check your system on my end. Okay to put you on a brief hold?

CASSIE

Nuh-uh.

A not-so-brief hold ensues, while PHONE TECH #5 hums and bops to the music.

PHONE TECH #5

Well, ma'am, the trouble seems to be on your end.

CASSIE
(sarcastically)

On my end! Of course.

PHONE TECH #5

I'll send a service technician right out to investigate. Okay?

CASSIE
(worried)

Not really. When can they get here?

PHONE TECH #5

Oh, very soon! Only a week or two.

CASSIE
(hysterical)

But you don't understand! My boss will have my head if I can't fix this paste function. I have so many emails to send and…

YOUR CALL IS IMPORTANT TO US

                PHONE TECH #5
                (cutting her off)
Yes, ma'am. (*beat*) Please hold for our customer care survey.

Visibly reading from a script.

Outstanding ratings let other customers know they'll get the tech support they need. Can I count on you for a five-star review?

(Use a sign or a slide that indicates "Three Weeks Later")

Cassie is in her living room. She has changed back to her sweatshirt. She puts on a mask. She stands in the living room facing the door.

HOME TECH wears a branded WiFi4U polo shirt and a branded cloth mask. He stands by the door facing toward Cassie.

SFX Doorbell

                CASSIE
Coming!

She walks to the front door, and the HOME TECH enters.

                HOME TECH
                (speaking through a mask)
Howdy, ma'am.

                CASSIE
                (muffled, speaking through a mask)
Howd... Hello. Are you here to fix my problem?

                HOME TECH
What? Can you speak up, ma'am? It's hard to hear you through that mask.

                CASSIE
                (raising her voice)
Is that better?

HOME TECH

Yes, ma'am. What is the issue?

CASSIE
(flabbergasted)

Don't you have it in your notes?

HOME TECH

Well, you know, sometimes it's like a game of telephone. By the time it gets to me, it's all distorted. So, I'd like you to tell me about it yourself. Can I have a seat?

He spreads out on a sofa, crosses his legs, and makes himself at home.

HOME TECH

Do you have any coffee? My coffee place was closed…

CASSIE goes into her kitchen and gets a mug of coffee.

HOME TECH does some stretches.

CASSIE

Here you go!

She hands him the mug.

HOME TECH

Thanks!

He takes the mug and then removes the mask.

CASSIE looks uncomfortable and moves away from him.

He sips the coffee.

CASSIE gives in and removes her mask too, careful to stay six feet away from him.

HOME TECH

So. Let's start at the very beginning…

YOUR CALL IS IMPORTANT TO US

                    CASSIE
                    (singing)

...a very good place to start!

                  HOME TECH

What?

                    CASSIE

Never mind. The paste function doesn't work in my email.

                  HOME TECH

Yup, that's what I read in the notes.

                    CASSIE

Then why did I have to repeat it? (*under her breath*) It's like "Groundhog Day"!

                  HOME TECH
                 (sips his coffee)

Hmmm. No paste function! That's very strange. That simply should not happen. I've never heard anything like this before!

He scratches his head as he considers the problem.

Tell you what — let me verify your identity...

                    CASSIE
                    (begging)

Please, no...

                  HOME TECH
                (fast but clear)

When did you buy the computer? Do you still have the receipt? Do you use an ergonomic keyboard? Does the issue happen when you use other browsers? Is it weather-dependent? Does it happen on your devices? Have you dreamt about this problem? Do you have a significant other? How many times a week do you work out? Do you grow your own vegetables? Can you mute yourself on Zoom? Do you regularly feed your sourdough starter?

> CASSIE
> (shaking her head in disbelief)

Seriously?

> HOME TECH

Have you tried using another browser at all, like Lifgig or Criskdiffles? They only take a few days each to set up.

> CASSIE
> (not again…)

Nooooo!

> HOME TECH
> (mansplaining)

Well, I was just telling my wife the other day, you know, Honey, none of the kids are using computers anymore. It's just devices and phones and apps, apps, apps. Imagine that! After all those years of computer this and computer that, computers are disappearing. Like dinosaurs! Our little grandson even uses a cell phone. That's the way we talk with him, especially now that we can't see him in person, with the pandemic and all. (*leans in*) You know, he said the cutest thing the other day, he said (*high, soft, baby voice*), "Gwanpa, I wanna go to the…"

CASSIE interrupts him, loudly clearing her throat

> HOME TECH

Yes, well. This is very unusual, ma'am. Let me look it up.

Takes out his phone and punches a few keys.

Nope, only one other reported case like this, back in 2018. Gee, I have no idea what to do. Why don't you ask your IT person?

> CASSIE

I thought YOU were my IT person!

> HOME TECH
> (pleasantly)

Right. (*beat*) Well, I'll just have to take it to the supreme, elevated, escalated, tech support guru. If SHE can't fix it, nobody can!

YOUR CALL IS IMPORTANT TO US

CASSIE
(yelling)
But I have to get this fixed RIGHT NOW, so I can make tomorrow's work deadline. Otherwise, I'll lose my job!

HOME TECH
(unruffled)
Don't know what to tell you, dear. Thanks for the coffee! Have an awesome day!

Pockets the phone, picks up his mask, and departs.

(Use a sign or a slide that indicates "Four Weeks Later")

CASSIE is in her neat, well-organized home office, wearing office casual.

SFX cellphone text ping

RECORDING
You have a customer waiting on hold.

CASSIE enters, sits down at her desk, straightens her posture, and puts on a headset.

CASSIE
(chirpy and calm)
Hello! It's a beautiful day here at WiFi4U! This is Cassie. I'll spell that for you: C as in Charlie, A as in Alpha, S as in Sierra, another S as in Sierra, I as in India, E as in Echo. I'm your brand-new tech support manager! Whom do I have the pleasure of speaking with?

She pantomimes happily chatting with a customer.

SFX upbeat music

END OF PLAY

COMEDIES FOR THE VIRTUAL STAGE

Production Notes:

Costumes:
CASSIE: Sweatshirt, sweatpants, office-casual top, with WiFi4U pin

PHONE TECHS: working-from-home clothing

HOME TECH: WiFi4U-branded cloth mask and polo shirt

Props:
Headsets & cellphones (CASSIE, PHONE TECHS #1-5)

Keyboard (CASSIE)

Knitting project, knitting needles (CASSIE)

Nail file (CASSIE)

Cereal bowl, crunchy cereal, spoon (PHONE TECH #4)

Cup of tea (PHONE TECH #4)

Pandemic mask (CASSIE)

Mugs of coffee – 2

SFX:
Dial tone, phone number tones, outgoing call ringing, click

Computer keyboard keys clicking

International call static

Rooster crowing

Doorbell

Cellphone ping

Music:
Twangy country music, very fast classical music, annoying Oldies hit, corny Christmas music, upbeat music

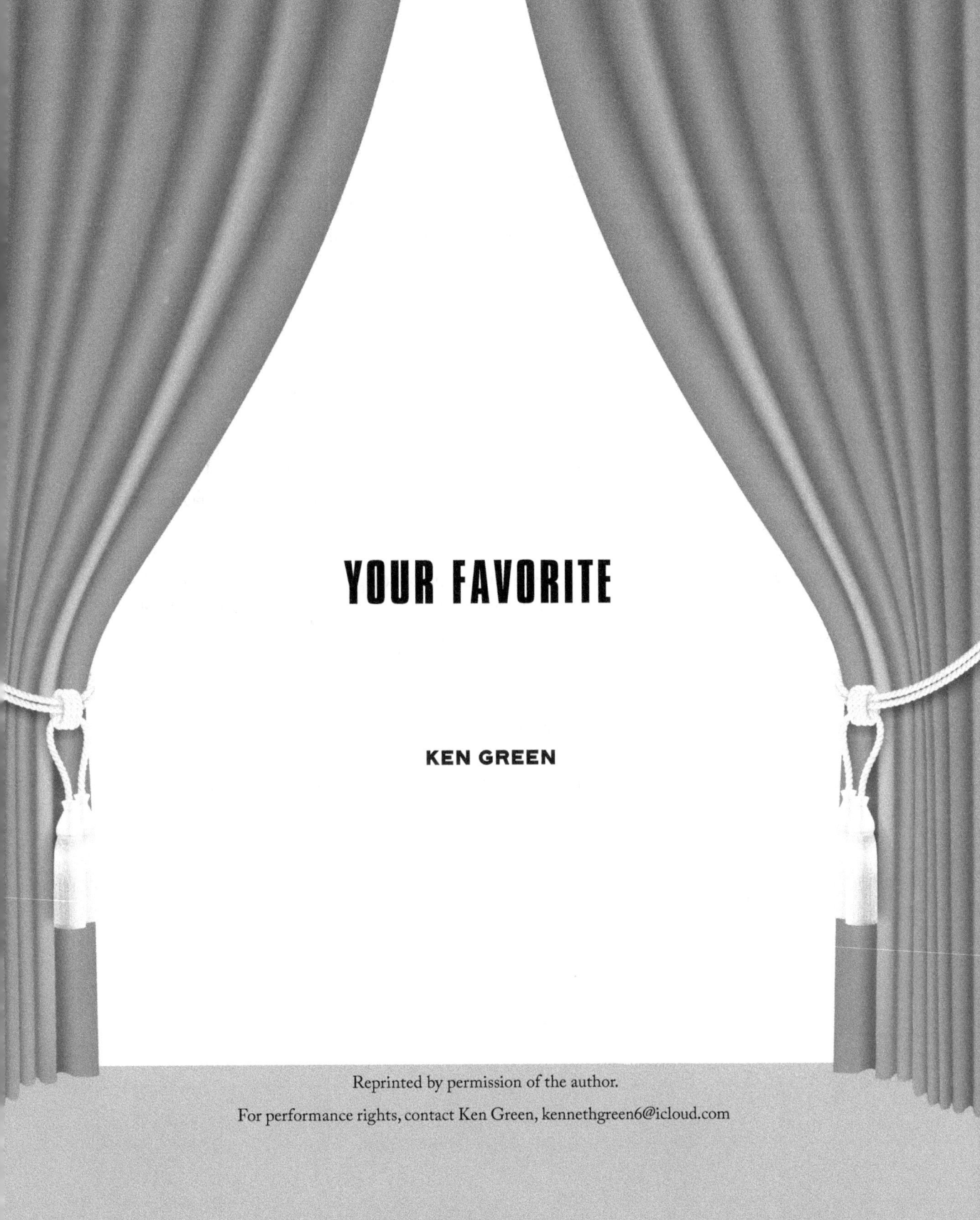

YOUR FAVORITE

KEN GREEN

Reprinted by permission of the author.
For performance rights, contact Ken Green, kennethgreen6@icloud.com

Synopsis

At a major art museum, an over-eager visitor finds out that not everyone is eager to share, and sometimes your thoughts are just YOUR thoughts. A play about art, museum guards, and whether scrambled eggs or yogurt go better with "Les Demoiselles d'Avignon."

Time

Present

Characters

VISITOR, male, late 50s, any race. Has a car salesman's confidence and conviviality. Mostly because he IS a car salesman. Assumes everyone's on the same page as him at all times.

GUARD, male, mid-50s, African American, or other person of color. Stoic. Has heard it all, extremely pragmatic, and annoyed easily. Doesn't understand people who think everyone should be on the same page.

Setting

Interior of a major international art museum in Chicago

NOTE: Ellipsis (...) at the end of a line means the next line is spoken before the first one completely ends.

Estimated run time

12 minutes

YOUR FAVORITE

Sunday afternoon at an internationally famous Chicago art museum. The halls are filled with people who want to be there, people who were dragged there, people who came there because we can't sit in front of the TV every goddam day, we need to DO something for a change, and... anyway...

In the corner of a gallery, a GUARD stands stoically, so much so that he might be mistaken for a piece of art himself. He is watching but not watching. An enthralled VISITOR walks the room, mouth agape at the paintings. He sees the GUARD and decides to strike up a conversation. The GUARD sees this too.

VISITOR
(to GUARD, brightly)

Hey. How's it going?...

GUARD
(small sigh, then flatly)

The museum was founded in 1879 in the aftermath of the Great Chicago Fire. It moved to its current location in 1893 for the World Columbian Exposi...

VISITOR

'Scuse me?

GUARD

Weren't you asking about the... (*realizes his mistake, is stoic again*) It's going fine.

VISITOR
(brightly)

I'm sure it is, I'm sure it is. (*pause*) So. (*He gestures around the museum*) Art, huh? Am I right?

GUARD
(flatly)

Well, this IS an art museum, so... you're right. This is art.

VISITOR
(laughing as heartily as the GUARD does not)

Funny. No, I meant more like... (*emphatic*) ART! Like, the history! The beauty! The... things!

> GUARD
> (flatly)

There ARE things here.

> VISITOR

Amazing. I mean, right over there, a Rembrandt. An honest-to-God Rembrandt. A Rem. Brandt! Like, look this way...
(Turns) ... nothing. Turn back... *(turns back)* Boom! Rembrandt!

> GUARD
> (flatly)

Yes. Boom.

> VISITOR

And Monet! I mean, c'mon, Monet? Get outta here!

> GUARD
> (droll)

Can't do that, sir. Working at the moment.

> VISITOR
> (oblivious)

Just... right there! A Monet. And a Cézanne. And a Goya. And...

> GUARD
> (getting to the point)

... and many other works of art in this... art museum.

> VISITOR

Exactly! I mean, I don't have to tell YOU... about... *(waits for GUARD to acknowledge)* Well, I mean, look at you.

> GUARD
> (unsure)

What am I doing?

> VISITOR

Well, you're here.

YOUR FAVORITE

GUARD
I do exist on this Earth.

VISITOR
No, I mean, you're HERE. In this museum.

GUARD
Well, "museum guard" isn't really a "work from home" position.

VISITOR
I mean you're lucky enough to stand right here all day...

GUARD
That's a very liberal interpretation of the word "lucky."

VISITOR
... and you get to SEE — up close — all this art. Every single day.

GUARD
Well, the art's over there, I'm here, so technically, yes, I get to see it every day.

VISITOR
(looking around again)
I mean, c'mon... Gauguin! Gauguin? An actual Gauguin? That's pretty mind-boggling.

GUARD
(a little puzzled)
As in amazing, overwhelming, incomprehensible? Seeing art in an art museum? That's "mind-boggling?"

VISITOR
Okay, maybe not Cleveland Browns-winning-the-Super-Bowl mind-boggling, but...

GUARD
So, some less mind-boggling level of mind-boggling.

VISITOR
(ignoring him)

I envy you, my friend.

GUARD
(confused)

I stand in one spot for five hours, my arches are as flat as a Kansas basketball court, and I actually have to tell people they can't put their hands on "A Sunday Afternoon on the Island of La Grande Jatte" by Georges Seurat. What part of that do you envy?

VISITOR
(ignoring again)

Now, I'll admit, I'm no art expert. I mean, I know some of the famous guys. Uh... Whistler. (*thinking*) Van Gogh, of course.

GUARD

Of course.

VISITOR

Um... (*thinking*) The melty watch guy.

GUARD

Salvador Dali?

VISITOR

No, the other guy.

GUARD

The other...?

VISITOR

But, overall, I don't know my ass from a Holbein in the ground. (*laughs at his own joke*)

GUARD

And you said you weren't an art expert.

YOUR FAVORITE

VISITOR
(seriously again)

But I do appreciate art, you know? I really do. I mean, sure, I own the second and third largest Honda dealerships in the Upper Midwest region and look out, Norm Jacobson's Honda Superstore, I'm gunning for you... (*getting somber*) But I also appreciate art. All this art? I appreciate it. I appreciate art. (*pause*) I'm appreciating it right now.

GUARD

And I'm sure the artists appreciate you appreciating their art. Or would if they weren't... dead?

VISITOR
(pause, then to GUARD)

Soooo... What about you?

GUARD

What about me what?

VISITOR

I mean... which one... (*gestures around the museum*)

GUARD

Which one... what?

VISITOR

Is your favorite?

GUARD

My favorite... what?

VISITOR

Your favorite pre-sweetened breakfast cereal. (*laughs*) C'mon, man, your favorite painting, of course. In this museum. The one that gets you... right here.

GUARD

You're grabbing your stomach.

VISITOR
Exactly. The one that makes your stomach all fluttery and your heart beat ten times faster.

GUARD
Sounds like pancreatitis. No, I don't...

VISITOR
(let's try this another way)
Okay, say you can take a painting home...

GUARD
That would require a LOT of paperwork.

VISITOR
Fine, we do the paperwork, bing bang boom, you take it home. Now, which one...

GUARD
(let's try this another way)
Look, there are too many to choose from, so I don't...

VISITOR
(interrupting excitedly)
Wait! The classics! I'm in the car business. It's my job to read people, and you (*thinking*) like the masters! Vermeer. Da Vinci. Michelangelo... no, Degas! I mean, who doesn't love freakin' Degas? C'mon...

GUARD
(to get him to shut up)
Sure, the masters...

VISITOR
(on second thought)
No, wait, you look more... abstract.

GUARD
I try not to slouch.

YOUR FAVORITE

VISITOR
(studying him)
You're more... modern. Probably a Kandinsky guy. Or... Man Ray! Yeah, Man Ray. Everybody loves Man Ray (*laughs*) Like that TV show with the guy and the wife...

GUARD
I got the joke.

VISITOR
But seriously, what I meant was what's your FAVORITE painting...

GUARD
(coldly)
I... Look, I'm trying not to be rude, but...

VISITOR
(afraid he's offended him)
What? You are NOT rude. You seem VERY patient. And reasonable. Patient and reasonable. Like a pope... or someone who works at a public television station. You're THAT patient and reasonable.

GUARD
Well, it comes in handy... like right now, in fact.

VISITOR
So, anyway, favorite painting... go!

GUARD
(*sigh*) Sorry, no.

VISITOR
No?

GUARD
Yes. No.

VISITOR
(confused)
So, wait, I ask, "favorite painting" and you...

GUARD
No.

VISITOR
(pause, thinking)
Is that the name of the artist or the painting, or...?

GUARD
No, that's just me talking. No.

VISITOR
(more confused)
I don't under... Look, I apologize if I said something wrong, and I... blame my white privilege?

GUARD
Your white privilege is fine. But just... no.

VISITOR
(assessing the situation)
Okay, so I ask your favorite painting, and you... "no"?

GUARD
Bingo.

VISITOR
But... "favorite painting." It's just a simple question. Just one person — me — asking another person...

GUARD
Me?

YOUR FAVORITE

VISITOR
Exactly. Asking a VERY simple question. I mean, "favorite painting." Pft. Barely even a question.

GUARD
Barely. But still a question, though. A little personal, too.

VISITOR
Personal? Naaaah. It's just "favorite painting." It's not like asking for your birthdate. Or for some of your urine.

GUARD
(confused)
Why would you want my urine?

VISITOR
To steal your DNA? I guess? I think you can do that with urine.

GUARD
Well, I'll give you all the urine you want.

VISITOR
So, you're okay with identity theft, but not with saying your favorite painting?

GUARD
Right. No.

VISITOR
(*pause*) Can I ask why?

GUARD
Sure.

A beat.

VISITOR
Ah. Okay, why?

GUARD
Because it doesn't matter.

VISITOR
(trying to comprehend)
You think your favorite painting doesn't matter?

GUARD
To me, sure. To someone else? Nope.

VISITOR
C'mon, man, of course, it matters. Your opinion on art matters. It's the... exchange of human ideas. Sharing viewpoints. Everybody's art opinion matters.

GUARD
(laughs)
Not really.

VISITOR
Of course, it does.

GUARD
The other day, someone said Van Gogh's "Starry Night" was the greatest painting ever...

VISITOR
(thinking)
I could see that. It's a classic. Like a beautiful dreamscape of...

GUARD
... because the title would also be a great stripper name.

VISITOR
Oh. Well... still, it's an opinion worth...

GUARD
Okay, fine, say I tell you my favorite painting. Then... what?

YOUR FAVORITE

VISITOR
(confused)
"What" what?

GUARD
What happens?

VISITOR
(thinking)
Well... You tell me your favorite painting, and *(thinking)* I don't know.

GUARD
Nothing happens.

VISITOR
Nothing? *(thinking)* Okay. Nothing, I guess.

GUARD
Exactly. Nothing happens. So, why bother asking?

VISITOR
Well, what's SUPPOSED to happen? We're just two people connecting, making conversation. It's like accepted museum protocol. You visit a museum, you ask the guard their favorite painting. *(pause)* It's probably an insult for me NOT to ask.

GUARD
Standing in an art museum, staring at some undefined point on the horizon, contemplating life, doesn't give me special insight into abstract impressionism. *(getting exasperated)* Fine, I tell you my favorite painting, you listen to me, and then you go, "Oh." Or "Nice." Or "Great."

VISITOR
Okay, so...

GUARD
And then... nothing. You go on with your day, I go on with mine, and whatever I said is forgotten like... *(snaps fingers)*. So, why bother?

VISITOR
Well, I... (*thinking*) I mean... Okay, maybe you're right.

GUARD
MAYBE I'm right?

VISITOR
Fine. You ARE right. My head's not gonna explode if you tell me your favorite painting... (*pause*) Which is...?

GUARD
Nope.

VISITOR
And I'm probably not gonna be sitting in some restaurant a month from now thinking, "Wow, I STILL can't believe that was his favorite painting."

GUARD
Exactly.

VISITOR
But, again, it's just one of those questions that people ask someone with a job like yours.

GUARD
Do you ask the kid tearing tickets at the movie theater what he thinks of Kurosawa, or do you just go sit down and eat your overpriced Red Twizzlers?

VISITOR
Why would I...

GUARD
Do you ask the guy at the security desk of the Empire State Building if he thinks Art Deco architecture is going to make a comeback?

VISITOR
Well, no, I...

YOUR FAVORITE

GUARD
So why ask ME about my favorite painting? Especially when people really don't care. (*getting worked up a bit*) All day long, people come here and demand...

VISITOR
Demand?

GUARD
Okay, "ask with unusual directness." They ask me my favorite painting. Like they're the only one to ever think of doing that. Like they're the first ones to come up with that question. You know, there are a million other things they could ask me. "What's it like working in a museum?" "Has anybody ever tried to steal a statue?" "Has anybody ever vomited on a painting?"

VISITOR
Wait, have they?

GUARD
I have no idea, but it's a more interesting question than "What's your favorite painting?" isn't it? You'd remember THAT answer. But all anyone wants to know is "favorite painting."

VISITOR
Are they at least nice about it?

GUARD
I had one guy report me for not answering the question. They had to explain it's not a job requirement. But over and over and over... people ask. (*pause*) You ever been asked the same question over and over and over?

VISITOR
Actually, yeah, but my mom stopped when I got married.

GUARD
Besides, "What's your favorite painting?" isn't a throwaway question. It's not something I can answer on a whim. Favorite painting... It's the result of time, thoughtful consideration. My entire life experience to that point. The places I've been, the people I've met... what I ate that day.

VISITOR
What you ate?

GUARD
Well, sure. I mean, I'm not gonna eat a big breakfast and go look at a Picasso, am I?

VISITOR
Yeah, that's... ridiculous?

GUARD
Exactly. Scrambled eggs, sausage, ham, toast, hash browns, and "Les Demoiselles d'Avignon"? Who does that?

VISITOR
No one... I guess.

GUARD
Of course not. Proto-cubism is more... fresh fruit, yogurt. Maybe muesli. Now, your big breakfast, that's post-impressionism. Your Paul Cezanne "Basket of Apples." Gaugin's "Two Tahitian Women." "The Boating Party" by Mary Cassatt. Stuff you can sink your teeth into.

VISITOR
What about... (*thinking*) a bagel and cream cheese?

GUARD
(not missing a beat)
Easy. Art Deco. Erté. Andre Maré. Claire Colinet. You know, soft, yet still a lot of structure.

VISITOR
(thinking, then...)
Kale salad!

GUARD
Pop art. I mean, Andy Warhol? Lichtenstein? Familiar, but with a little spin. Kale salad for sure.

YOUR FAVORITE

VISITOR

You might have a point. Once, I had a bowl of chili before a Basquiat exhibition. Couldn't enjoy it at all. (*pause*) You've got some well-thought-out ideas on art. And, I guess, food, too.

GUARD

Which is why I don't talk about my favorite painting. People don't actually want to know. They don't care about my thoughts on why Henri de Toulouse-Lautrec would have been a MUCH different artist had he been six-one instead of four-eight.

VISITOR

I imagine the floor wouldn't have been such a big part of his work. (*pause*) Look, I gotta apologize.

GUARD
(feeling guilty)

No, you don't... (*pause*) I just hate that it's assumed I should share what's in my brain with anyone who passes by.

VISITOR

I get it. I mean, your favorite painting is YOUR favorite painting. Not mine. People should respect that. (*pause*) Apologies for sticking my nose in your brain.

GUARD

A slightly disturbing thought, but I get it. (*pause*) Thanks.

VISITOR

Look, I'm gonna leave you to whatever is in your head. You have a nice day. (*pause*) Or just... have whatever kind of day you want to have.

GUARD

Thanks. You, too. Have a... whatever day.

VISITOR walks away, and then GUARD calls after him.

GUARD
Hey! (*pause*) Um... "Greyed Rainbow."

VISITOR
What?

GUARD
"Greyed Rainbow." Jackson Pollock.

VISITOR
What about it?

GUARD
My, uh... favorite painting. Abstract expressionism. Kinda out there, but I like it. I see something different every time I look at it. Second floor. In Contemporary Art. If you wanna look at it.

VISITOR
Thanks. I'll check it out. (*pause*) Wait, I had a turkey sandwich for lunch...

GUARD
You'll be okay.

VISITOR
Thanks again.

GUARD
Anytime. (*pause*) Well, not ANY time, but... you know.

    VISITOR leaves.

END OF PLAY

EDITORS

Janet R. Carpman, PhD, is *PlayZoomers'* co-founder, Executive Director, and Board President. She produces all *PlayZoomers'* shows with Mary Ann Nichols, casts many, and directs on occasion. Jan also founded and currently produces the *PlayZoomers* "Act Me a Story" early childhood literacy video program in conjunction with the Michigan nonprofit, Washtenaw Promise. Music and theatre (and musical theatre) have been her lifelong passions, indulged by many years of singing, acting, directing, stage managing, and more with various organizations and community theatres. While living in Michigan, Jan co-founded a song-and-dance troupe specializing in vintage American popular music and was a producer, performer, and Board President for nearly twenty-five years. Now based in Boston, she is also an architectural sociologist and wayfinding expert, writer, speaker, and co-author of two award-winning books, *Design that Cares: Planning Health Facilities for Patients & Visitors*, and *Directional Sense: How to Find Your Way Around*. carpmanwayfinding.com   playzoomers.org

Mary Ann Nichols is *PlayZoomers'* co-founder and Literary Manager. She curates, shapes, and produces each *PlayZoomers'* season in partnership with Jan Carpman. She often casts shows and occasionally directs and acts. As Literary Manager, she manages a team of script vetters who help evaluate script submissions. Mary is a radio professional, actor, voiceover artist, director, teacher, musician, and acting coach who has worked at nearly every level of the craft. Her extensive professional radio career began as a classical announcer/programmer at WGMS (Washington, DC) and WCRB (Boston, Massachusetts). She then worked as a news anchor and local/national voice of underwriting at WBUR, Boston's NPR News station. Credits include audiobook narration and on-camera commercial work; many of her audiobooks are available through the National Library Service of the Library of Congress.

CONTRIBUTORS

John Busser (Playwright, *A First-Draft Second-Rate Love Story*) is an actor/writer/graphic artist from Avon, Ohio. He is the co-runner of Cleveland Public Theatre's writers' workshop, The Dark Room, which helps playwrights test-drive new work. He has written over 120 short plays, some of which have been produced throughout the US, Canada, the UK, India, and Australia. Some of his more well-known works include: *Children's Letters to Satan (and Other Horrible Scribblings),* a collection of seven of his original plays, which is available from Next Stage Press. His award-winning short play, *Obstacle,* was made into a film that has played festivals across the globe. His sci-fi dramedy *Taylor-Made* premiered on Broken Arts Entertainment audio series, *The Future,* and garnered over four thousand views. John is a 2025 winner of the *PlayZoomers'* Thomas W. Stephens Playwriting Competition for his play, *Old Wives' Tail.* He writes his nonsense in lieu of having to perform community service.

Janet R. Carpman, PhD (Playwright, *Your Call is Important to Us*) (bio above)

CONTRIBUTORS

Patricia Connelly (Playwright, *The Holiest of Sacraments*) is an award-winning playwright and director. Her full-length plays include *Night Sky, Heartland, Around the Snake Turn, Princess Margaret, The Penny or the Stone, What Happens in This Town, All the Sins of My Past Life*, and *Harriet*. She has also written one-act plays. She has a Master of Arts in Theatre from the University of New Mexico and an MFA in Creative Writing (Playwriting) from Goddard College. She is co-founder and producer of Pipeline Playwrights, a member of the Dramatists Guild of America, and a proud member of Honor Roll.

Nicky Denovan (Playwright, *Armchair Critic*) is a UK playwright whose work has been performed across the world — from New York to New Zealand, Sydney to South India. Nicky topped the British Animation Film Festival's Lottie Reiniger List, winning Best Screenplay. She is a previous winner of Pint-Sized Plays, Short + Sweet Theatre, and TakeTen Chesil Theatre New Writing Festival. For screenwriting, she is a three-time ScreenCraft quarterfinalist, a two-time Annual Fade In Awards semi-finalist, a finalist in the Los Angeles International Screenplay Awards, and a best script winner in the Animotion Film Festival. Nicky's work has been featured on BBC Radio, at the Edinburgh Fringe, INK, and Latitude Festivals, and in books published in the UK and the US.

Lisa Dellagiarino Feriend (Playwright, *Drummer Boy*) is an award-winning playwright, a member of the Dramatists Guild, and President of the Board of Arts For All, a New York City nonprofit bringing accessible artistic opportunities to children who face barriers to exploring the arts. She has developed work with Bay Street Theatre in Sag Harbor, New York; Gulfshore Playhouse in Naples, Florida; The Bechdel Group in New York City; The Depot for New Play Readings; and the Chicago Women's Theatre Alliance, among others. Lisa has a BFA in Film & TV from NYU and two kids who are disappointed that she doesn't write plays about dinosaurs. arts-for-all.org

Seth Freeman (Playwright, *Imperfectly Frank*) is a playwright, a writer/producer for television, a journalist, and an educator. He co-founded the Chamber Theatre in Berkeley, California, and his short plays have been presented at over three hundred theatres and festivals around the world. He created the television series *Lincoln Heights*, and his work in TV has been recognized with multiple Emmys, Golden Globes, and numerous other honors. His articles appear in *The New York Times, Southern Theatre Magazine, The Wall Street Journal*, and other periodicals. In 2019, he earned a Master's degree in Public Health. He dedicates time to initiatives involving education, healthcare, and human rights.

Sam Graber (Playwright, *Talkback*) has written plays staged by theatres across the country. *The Watchers* was awarded the 2016 Broadway Producer List (New York City). *Shooter* received its world premiere at *Theaterlab* before embarking on a European tour with the original New York City cast. He teaches classes at The Playwrights' Center. His work has been published by Smith & Kraus, Original Works, and Dramatic Publishing. He lives outside Minneapolis, Minnesota, where the temperature is currently 406 degrees colder than wherever you are.

Ken Green (Playwright, *Your Favorite*) currently resides in Boston's Dorchester neighborhood. His plays include *In The Back/On The Floor*, produced by Chicago's *Stage Left Theater* in the Spring of 2023; *July 5th*, a full-length audio drama on the life of Frederick Douglass, commissioned by New York City's Ensemble for the Romantic Century; *The F&L at 1330*, as part of Moonbox Productions' Boston New Works Festival 2023; and *The Charles Lenox Experience*, commissioned and produced in 2020 by New Repertory Theater in Watertown, Massachusetts. Other plays include *The Campaign* and *… And Then There's Aaron Burr*, all featured at the Boston Theater Marathon.

CONTRIBUTORS

Greg Hatfield (Playwright, *Curtain Call*) has been writing comedy for nearly five decades. A published author, director, and contributor, his plays have been performed throughout the US and in London, England. His play cycle, *The Cabot Comedies*, is published by Next Stage Press. He is a member of the Dramatists Guild. His plays are listed on New Play Exchange. More at greghatfield.com.

Lenny Hort (Playwright, *Chemistry Date*) is a member of the Dramatists Guild and The Forge play development lab at Hudson Theatre Works. His musical, *Pirates in the Gazebo!*, won a BMI Foundation Award for outstanding creative achievement. His plays, including *Chemistry Date, Grave Offense, Julius C-SPAN,* and *Origin Story,* have been featured on radio, YouTube™, and Zoom™, and performed in a dozen states. *A Little Something About My Powers* was voted Best Play at the Equity Library Theater of New York Virtual Play Festival. lennyhort.com

Nick Maynard (Playwright, *A Snake with a Ladder*) is a multi-award-winning writer and artist living and working in Manchester, England. His works have been performed in London, Memphis, Chicago, and New York City, and appear in several periodicals and anthologies. His first novel, *Cripple,* is available on Amazon.

COMEDIES FOR THE VIRTUAL STAGE

James McLindon (Playwright, *Santa Noir*) is a member of the Nylon Fusion Theatre Company in New York. His plays have been produced or developed at theatres across the US and around the world, including the O'Neill National Playwrights Conference (selection and six-time semi-finalist), Lark, PlayPenn, Edinburgh Fringe Festival, hotINK Festival, Irish Repertory, CAP21, Samuel French Festival, Victory Gardens, Hudson Stage Company, Abingdon, New Repertory Theatre, Lyric Stage, Detroit Rep, Great Plains Theatre Conference, Seven Devils, Telluride Playwrights Festival, Ashland New Plays Festival, Boston Playwrights Theatre, Colony Theatre, Theatricum Botanicum, Circus Theatricals, and Arkansas Rep. They have been published by Dramatic Publishing, Smith & Kraus, Brooklyn Publishing, Applause Books, Next Stage Press, and Original Works Publishing.

John Minigan (Playwright, *The Noir Before Christmas*) is a recent Massachusetts Cultural Council Artist Fellow in Playwriting. He's been commissioned to create new works by Gloucester Stage Company, Concert Theatre Works, Lyric Stage Company of Boston, and Hey Jonté Productions. His solo adaptation of *The Legend of Sleepy Hollow* won the BroadwayWorld Best New Play Award and was an Elliot Norton Outstanding New Script nominee. *Out of the Scorpion's Nest* (formerly known as *Queen of Sad Mischance*) won the Kennedy Center's Royer Award, and *Noir Hamlet* was an EDGE Media Best of Boston Theater selection. John teaches at Emerson College and serves as Boston's Dramatists Guild Ambassador. johnminigan.com

Morey Norkin (Playwright, *Can You Hear Me Now?*) is a retired technical writer/proposal manager from Maryland now living in Japan. After many years of involvement in Annapolis-area community theaters, he took up playwriting in 2019. Besides three productions with *PlayZoomers*, Morey's work has also been produced by the Jewish Plays Project, Sydney's Short + Sweet Festival, GreenMan Theatre Troupe, ATC Studios, Grand Drama

CONTRIBUTORS

and Comedy Club, Dominion Stage, Colonial Players, and podcasts by Broken Arts Entertainment and Theatrical Shenanigans. Morey's plays are found at New Play Exchange.

Steven Otfinoski (Playwright, *The Audition, A Horse! A Horse!*) has had many plays — both short and long — produced across the US and internationally. *The Audition*, which appears in this anthology, won the Best Script Award at the Short + Sweet Festival in Sydney, Australia. Six of his plays have been performed at the National Arts Club in Manhattan. Other plays have been produced by the Magnetic Theatre, Asheville, North Carolina; Lake Shore Players, Minneapolis, Minnesota; and TheatreWorks, New Milford, Connecticut. Steve earned his MFA in Creative Writing from Fairfield University, where he teaches English. He is also the author of more than two hundred young adult books and reviews theatre in the Berkshires for the *Journal of American Drama and Theatre*. He is a proud member of the Dramatists Guild.

R.A. Pauli (Playwright, *Tree #2*) began writing plays in 2009 while working as a Senior Writer at Hallmark Cards in Kansas City, Missouri. To date, he has enjoyed live and streaming productions and staged readings of forty-one of his plays, ranging from one-minute-play extravaganzas to ten-minute-play festivals, to full-length presentations, by forty-nine theatres in twenty states and Australia. He has won many audience-favorite and best-play awards and is a member of the Dramatists Guild of America. When not writing plays, he composes music, plays keyboard in his neighborhood band, The Rockin' Chairs, and embarrasses himself weekly on the tennis court.

Cary Pepper (Playwright, *I've Got a Bun*) has had work presented throughout the US and internationally. Most recently, *From the Hoot* won the Playwrights First Award; *Dolly Gets Her Shot* was his third production by Drip Action Theatre (UK); *House of the Holy Moment* marked Cary's fourth appearance in the Newmarket International Festival of One Act Plays (Canada); and *What Do They Want?* made him the first playwright to be included three times in the St. Louis Actors' Studio's LaBute New Theater Festival. Cary is a member of the Dramatists Guild and a four-time contributor to Applause Books' *Best American Short Plays* series.

Curt Strickland (Playwright, *Speed Dating*) is a Boston-area playwright. Inspired by August Wilson, Curt is finishing up his fifth play in a ten-play opus on America, each play set in a different decade. You can view his other plays at New Play Exchange. Curt was awarded Best Play by the William Faulkner Literary Playwriting Competition for his play, *1968*. He recently published a book, *Democracy Under Siege: Essays on the Trump Years (2017-2024)*. In 2020, Curt received a double lung transplant, an event that had profound effects on both his writing and his life.

Trevor Suthers (Playwright, *Almost Perfect*) is a UK resident. He has had over eighty original works produced, ranging from monologues to musicals, full-length plays, one-act plays, and sketch shows, in every kind of venue and numerous non-theatre spaces. He has written for British TV Soaps *Coronation Street* and *EastEnders*. His plays have been staged, broadcast, and live-streamed in the US, with many published online. He is the founder of award-winning JB Shorts, Manchester's most popular fringe theatre event, presenting six short plays by experienced TV writers (biennially). It returns in 2025 for a twenty-fifth season. He has also written numerous plays for children and young people that are regularly performed globally.

ACKNOWLEDGMENTS

Thanks to the playwrights whose work we include in this anthology. We applaud their abilities to imaginatively and humorously express some of the messiness of being human.

PlayZoomers has been fortunate to work with scores of playwrights, directors, designers, actors, and others who have helped us develop and grow our online theatre company. We're grateful to all of them.

Our Literary Committee vets scripts that arrive by the hundreds over the virtual transom. Thank you, Duchess Dale, Nancy Dydak, AnnJ Gumbinner, Patti Allis Mengers, Joshua Secunda, Scott Sedar, Rachel Rycerz, Alice Simon, Barry Weinberg, and Lisa White.

Isidore Neubecker (Assistant Tech Director), Laura Hubbard (Website Administrator), Taiwo Aloba (Production Associate), Pierce Stephan (Social Media Manager), and Mona Bapat ("Act Me a Story" Supervising Director) help fuel our company's engine.

Past and present *PlayZoomers* Board members, including Audrey Appleby, Joel Bresler, Duchess Dale, George Dougherty, Gary Giurbino, Morris Schorr, Joshua Secunda, and the late Thomas W. Stephens, have guided and supported the company since its inception.

Graphic Designer Kathleen Murphy has provided creative and evocative images for virtual backgrounds and videos, as well as beautiful designs for posters and playbills. Technical Director Doug MacDougall has advised us on how to best use video conferencing technology and integrate curated royalty-free music and sound effects. He has created helpful bells-and-whistles, including publicity trailers, Intro/Outro videos, preshow presentations, scene transition/special effects videos, and edited/archived production recordings.

The work of all these talented people would be for naught without an enthusiastic audience that eagerly tunes in to our live, online performances.

Janet R. Carpman
Executive Director,
Founding Producer,
PlayZoomers, Inc.

Mary Ann Nichols,
Literary Manager,
Founding Producer,
PlayZoomers, Inc.